GCSE RELIGIOUS STUDIES

AN INTRODUCTION TO CHRISTIAN ETHICS

Truth

NEXT EXIT

Colourpoint
Educational

Rewarding Learning

Juliana Gilbride

ISBN: 978 1 906578 36 7

First Edition
First Impression

Layout and design: Colourpoint Books
Printed by: W&G Baird, Antrim

Colourpoint
Educational

Colourpoint Books
Colourpoint House
Jubilee Business Park
21 Jubilee Road
Newtownards
County Down
Northern Ireland
BT23 4YH

Tel: 028 9182 6339
Fax: 028 9182 1900
E-mail: info@colourpoint.co.uk
Web site: www.colourpoint.co.uk

The Author

Juliana Gilbride, B.Ed (Hons), M.Ed, was part of a team of teachers who revised the Religious Studies GCSE Specification for CCEA (for first teaching in 2009). She is a Revisor for GCSE Religious Studies for CCEA, and has fifteen years experience of teaching Religious Studies in Northern Ireland.

Acknowledgements

Thanks are due to a number of people who helped with this book: Fransuer Mukula for his contribution to Chapter 4; Accord and Relate; and those who supplied photographs including Martin Gilbride and Marion Dempsey. Special thanks go to Donna Finlay (CCEA); Joan Williams (CCEA); Philip Barnes (CCEA); Sheila Johnson and Rachel Irwin at Colourpoint for their guidance throughout the writing process; Martin, Tom and Kate Gilbride for their patience; and to Teresa O'Callaghan for her encouragement and support.

Picture credits

Cover image: iStockphoto

Luke Brown: 50 (top left)

G Cornelius: 32

D DeMarsico: 60 (left)

Marion Dempsey: 48

K Forstner: 8

Juliana Gilbride: 49, 50 (bottom left)

Martin Gilbride: 31

Rachel Irwin: 76

iStockphoto: 9, 10, 14, 19, 22, 26, 27 (left), 29, 42, 44, 45, 47, 55 (both), 58 (left), 59, 61, 64, 69, 75, 78 (left)

Norman Johnston: 41

Wesley Johnston: 67 (both)

Rachel Kinnaird: 50 (bottom right)

Fransuer Mukula: 61

Shutterstock: 71

US Federal Government: 56 (right)

CONTENTS

SP09

This symbol denotes questions taken from the CCEA 2009 specimen paper.

 For your folder    In A Group   Further Thinking

Chapter 1

PERSONAL AND FAMILY ISSUES

● THE MEANING AND PURPOSE OF SEXUAL RELATIONSHIPS

WHAT IS A SEXUAL RELATIONSHIP?

At some point during the teenage years people develop sexual feelings. This means that they may find another person physically attractive, think about them a lot and want to spend time with them. Perhaps some people in your class have a boyfriend or girlfriend that they are 'seeing' or 'going out with'. They may even say that they are in love and cannot imagine life without each other.

A sexual relationship is one where two people who are best friends (usually a man and a woman) agree (consent) to have sex on a regular basis. Another term for such a relationship between a man and a woman is a **heterosexual relationship** and it usually applies to adults. Most people wait until they are older or even married before they have a sexual relationship. However, in today's society there is a lot of pressure on people who are physically attracted towards each other to have sex, even if they are young teenagers or do not know each other all that well. The legal age for having sex in Northern Ireland, known as 'the age of consent', is 16.

A **homosexual relationship** is one where two men are attracted to each other or two women are attracted to each other. A woman who has same-sex relationships is called a lesbian. Some people are sexually attracted to both men and women. They are called bisexual. In 1994 the age of homosexual consent was lowered to 18 (Section 145 Criminal Justice and Public Order Act, 1994).

CHRISTIAN OPINIONS ON HOMOSEXUALITY

Christian viewpoints on homosexuality vary from outright condemnation to complete acceptance. Christians who totally condemn homosexuality point to Paul's writings in the New Testament. For example:

> "Surely you know that the wicked will not possess God's Kingdom. Do not fool yourselves; people who are immoral or who worship idols or are adulterers or homosexual perverts…"
>
> 1 Corinthians 6:9

Other Christians are more sympathetic and claim that this applies only to a homosexual 'act' and not the 'condition' of being homosexual. They argue that as long as a person with homosexual tendencies does not act on their feelings then they are not condemned. At the other extreme are people who believe it is all right to be a practicing homosexual and a Christian. This view is supported by groups such as The Lesbian and Gay Christian Movement and The Evangelical Fellowship for Lesbian and Gay Christians.

WHAT DO THE CHURCHES SAY?
Look at the following information and summarise the opinion of each Christian denomination.

The Catholic Church	"Homosexuality refers to relations between men or between women who experience an exclusive or predominant sexual attraction toward persons of the same sex…Its psychological genesis remains largely unexplained. Basing itself on Sacred Scripture, which presents homosexual acts as acts of grave depravity, tradition has always declared that 'homosexual acts are intrinsically disordered'…Under no circumstances can they be approved…men and women who have deep-seated homosexual tendencies…must be accepted with respect, compassion, and sensitivity. Every sign of unjust discrimination in their regard should be avoided. These persons are called to fulfill God's will in their lives and, if they are Christians, to unite to the sacrifice of the Lord's Cross the difficulties they may encounter from their condition. Homosexual persons are called to chastity." *Catechism of the Catholic Church*
The Church of Ireland	The Anglican Church (which includes the Church of Ireland) is more controversial when it comes to issues about homosexuality. • A resolution was passed at the Lambeth Conference in 1998, stating that homosexual acts are "incompatible with Scripture". However, it also said this policy would not be the final word. • In 2003, the Church of England was prepared to appoint as bishop, Jeffrey John, a priest living in a celibate domestic partnership with another man. Many Anglicans were outraged and the priest decided not to accept the appointment. • Many Church of Ireland parishes, particularly in Northern Ireland, are opposed to homosexual practice.
The Presbyterian Church	"Many teenagers experience same sex attractions. For most these do not linger but are part of their sexual development. For others their sexual development can be arrested by various factors in their upbringing including close family relationships and family breakdown. In our culture, that includes the promotion of alternative sexualities. This can result in some young people being confused about their sexuality. They may need help to understand and work through deeper-seated insecurities, issues of forgiveness, gender acceptance and self-acceptance before they can come to terms with their sexual identity." *Pastoral Guidelines – Homosexuality, Social Issues and Resources Panel*

FURTHER THINKING

Find out what you can about the opinions of the Baptist Church and the Methodist Church on homosexuality.

IN A GROUP

Summarise in point form the different church opinions about homosexuality.

CIVIL PARTNERSHIPS

The Civil Partnership Act 2004 came into operation on 5 December 2005. It allows a same-sex couple to register as civil partners of each other. The first set of civil partnership ceremonies for gay couples in the UK were held in Northern Ireland.
Shannon Sickles and Grainne Close were one of the couples taking part in civil ceremonies at Belfast City Hall.

Around 30 protesters were also there to show they disagreed with the union. Miss Close commented: "We just want to say that this is a very privileged position we are in this morning and for us this is about making a choice." Her partner, added: "This is about making a choice to have our civil rights acknowledged and protected…We feel very privileged and blessed to be here doing this and look forward to having a wonderful day."

PRE-MARITAL SEX

People are a lot more willing to discuss sexual issues than they were in the past. We are bombarded with sexual images on television, in newspapers and magazines and in advertising. Most teenage magazines are full of articles about sex, and problem pages are full of letters which suggest that the teenagers who read the magazine are all sexually active. You may be left wondering if there is something wrong with you if you are still a virgin by the time you are 18.

Christians believe that sexual intercourse is a sacred act which should take place only in a committed marriage relationship. The act of never having sex is called 'chastity'. Christians believe all people who are not married should be 'chaste'. All of the main Christian churches agree with this.

> **The Presbyterian Church:**
> "Ideally God meant sex to be enjoyed in the context of the full commitment of marriage. It is the physical expression of the deeper reality of two becoming one in marriage."
>
> *Contraception, Social Issues & Resources Committee*

> **The Church of Ireland:**
> "We believe that human sexuality is a wonderful gift from God and, at a time in life when they are most aware of this gift, we would urge that young people question any behaviour that devalues this gift, or which hinders its fulfillment within the context of marriage."
>
> *General Synod, 1992*

> **The Catholic Church**
> "Fornication is carnal union between an unmarried man and an unmarried woman. It is gravely contrary to the dignity of persons and of human sexuality which is naturally ordered to the good of spouses and the generation and education of children."
>
> *Catechism of the Catholic Church*

Christians argue against sex before marriage for a number of reasons:

- The Bible teaches that sex should take place only within marriage: *"that is why a man leaves his father and mother and is united with his wife, and they become one"* (Genesis 2:24).
- Avoiding sex before marriage prevents an unwanted pregnancy outside marriage.
- Avoiding sex before marriage lessens the risk of getting a sexually transmitted disease. The Presbyterian Church argues: "For those who are married, faithfulness to one's marriage partner is the norm. Monogamous heterosexual marriage is still the best defence against sexually transmitted disease and especially HIV/AIDS".
- People can become emotionally hurt by having sex in a relationship which is not a life-long commitment. When the relationship ends they can be left feeling devalued and used.

SINGLE LIFE

In our society the majority of people choose to get married or to live with someone at some point in their lives. However, there is a minority who deliberately choose not to enter into a relationship but to remain single. Some of the reasons for this are:

- **Religious reasons** – Some religious orders ask their members not to have sexual relations of any kind so that they can devote themselves to God and the service of others, as Christ did. Priests and nuns are examples. Such people take a vow of 'celibacy'. They regard the Church as their family and don't want any distractions from their duties.
- **Still looking** – some people are single because they have not found a person that they want to spend their lives with.
- **Divorce** – a divorced person may choose not to become involved in another relationship. Perhaps they are too hurt by what has happened to them. Children may be involved and they think it would be unfair to them to become involved with somebody else.
- **Death of a partner** – their partner has died and they do not want to become involved with anyone else.

IN A GROUP

- **Can you think of any other reasons?**
- **In the Bible Paul recommends the single life. Read 1 Corinthians 7:32–33 and copy out the main points of Paul's advice.**

The Christian Church has contrasting opinions about marriage for the clergy. The Roman Catholic Church recommends that priests should remain single because it "enables them to give themselves to God alone with an undivided heart in a remarkable manner" (The Catholic Congregation for the Doctrine of the Faith, *Persona Humana* 7). A number of people argue that priests should be allowed to marry. They point to the fall in the number of young Catholic men who want to become priests.

IN A GROUP

Discuss the following opinions of people concerning marriage for priests. In a table write down the points that you agree with and those you disagree with:

Damien:
"A lot of boys follow in their father's footsteps when it comes to a choice of career. My Dad is a builder and that's what I am now. And my uncle is a teacher and his son is now training to be one. If priests were allowed to marry and have children, not only would more men of faith be attracted to the priesthood but more boys would want to be like their dads by becoming priests when they grow up."

Sean:
"I think it's right that priests can't marry. It sets them apart from the rest of us. You know they must be really committed to God because of the sacrifice they make. If any married man could become a priest there would be a fall in standards."

Gary:
"In the Protestant denominations ministers and pastors are allowed to marry. They are still very much respected as men of God. They also have personal experience of married life and know more about the challenges and difficulties of marriage. This means they can relate more to the ordinary people in their congregations."

Majella
"I don't know what all the fuss is about. If women were allowed to be priests then there wouldn't be a fall in numbers of people wanting to be priests. I don't think we should be arguing for priests to get married but for women to be priests."

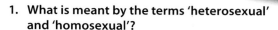

FOR YOUR FOLDER

1. What is meant by the terms 'heterosexual' and 'homosexual'?
2. What does the church teach about sex before marriage?
3. Do you think that sex should take place only between married heterosexual couples?
4. Why might some Christians protest against the legality of civil partnerships?
5. Why do some people decide to remain single?
6. "The Catholic Church should allow priests to get married." Do you agree or disagree? Give reasons for your answer.

MARRIAGE

Marriage is a social, religious and spiritual union of individual people. Usually a couple are engaged, have been 'going out' together or 'seeing each other' for a while when they decide to get married. This means they want to make a commitment to each other for the rest of their lives. The ceremony that marks the beginning of marriage is usually called a wedding.

When you think of a wedding you may imagine a church wedding with a bride dressed in an expensive white dress, with lots of bridesmaids, a fancy reception in a big hotel followed by an exciting honeymoon abroad. However, a lot of people choose to get married in a registry office. In the UK and Ireland marriages can also take place at a building approved for civil marriage. The Catholic Church, however, does not recognise a marriage that takes place outside the church.

Most people probably think that they might get married at some point in their lives. However, some couples decide not to get married at all. They argue that they do not need a marriage certificate to prove how committed they are to each other.

WHAT THE BIBLE SAYS ABOUT MARRIAGE

Marriage is sacred – God created marriage and intends men and women to become 'one' through marriage (Genesis 2:21–24).

Marriage should be exclusive – The Ten Commandments condemn adultery (Exodus 20:14). The selfishness of adultery is highlighted in the story of David and Bathsheba, where their adultery led to more sin with the murder of Bathsheba's husband (2 Samuel 11:12–25).

Marriage involves give and take – In Paul's letter to the church at Corinth he advises: *"A man should fulfill his duty as a husband, and a woman should fulfill her duty as a wife, and each should satisfy the other's needs"* (1 Corinthians 7:3–4). Partners should be prepared to put each other's life before their own.

Marriage should be built on love and respect – In Paul's letter to Ephesus he compared the love between a man and a woman to the love which Christ has for his church (Ephesians 5:25–33).

THE CHRISTIAN WEDDING CEREMONY

Biblical teaching on marriage is reflected in the Christian wedding ceremony. A ceremony can vary from one denomination to another but there are certain important features common to them all.

Introduction and declaration of purpose

The priest or minister will give a short homily or sermon on the importance and purpose of marriage.

The Vows

These are required by law although the wording may change from church to church. A couple repeats the marriage vows to each other during the marriage ceremony. Some couples make up their own vows that are particularly special to them but most people use the following words:

▶

"To have and to hold from this day forward; for better for worse; for richer, for poorer; in sickness and in health; to love and to cherish; till death do us part."

Exchange of rings
Rings are exchanged as a symbol of the promise of unending love and the exclusive commitment which each partner is making.

Warning
The Priest or minister quotes Jesus' words:

"Man must not separate, then, what God has joined together."

Mark 10:9

Pronouncement
In some denominations it is stated that the couple are now married.

Signing of the register
This is a legal requirement in which a couple (and witnesses) sign a register. At a later stage they receive a marriage certificate. Many ordained priests and ministers are licensed Registrars and are authorised to issue marriage certificates. If they are not then a state Registrar must be present.

WHAT THE CHURCHES SAY ABOUT MARRIAGE

IN A GROUP

The following church statements highlight the beliefs that marriage is sacred; should be exclusive and permanent; and is for the purpose of having children. In a group read each statement and place them in the most appropriate box on a copy of the table opposite:

A "Marriage is a life-long partnership of man and wife with absolute faithfulness the one to the other."

'Getting Married', the Presbyterian Church

B "According to the teaching of Christ, marriage is a life-long union in body, mind and spirit, of one man and one woman. It is his will that in marriage the love of man and woman should be fulfilled in the wholeness of their life together, in mutual companionship, helpfulness and care. By the help of God this love grows and deepens with the years."

From the Methodist Marriage Service

C "The intimate community of life and love which constitutes the married state has been established by the Creator and endowed by him with its own proper laws…God himself is the author of marriage."

Roman Catholic Church, *Gaudium et Spes*, 48.1

D "Christian marriage has a two-fold purpose – fellowship and parenthood. Permanence in the union is an essential condition. It both expresses and develops not only constancy in affection, but also spiritual qualities of trust, faithfulness, mutual consideration, reverence and love."

Methodist Conference, 1980

E "We believe in the sanctity of marriage and that marriage was created by God and that the only legitimate form of marriage is between one man and one woman."

'Our Beliefs', Trinity Presbyterian Church, Bangor

F "In every age up to the present it was taken for granted that marriage was not simply a matter for the couple themselves but concerned their families and society. Husband and wife begin a new family, a

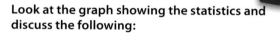

unit of society which both supports and is supported by the community as a whole…One of the functions of marriage is to provide a stable family unit, within the wider community, in which children can be born and nurtured."

Church of Ireland Marriage Council

G "Children are the supreme gift of marriage and contribute greatly to the good of the parents themselves. God himself said: 'It is not good that man should be alone," and "from the beginning [he] made them male and female'; wishing to associate them in a special way in his own creative work, God blessed man and woman with the words: 'Be fruitful and multiply.' Hence, true married love and the whole structure of family life which results from it, without diminishment of the other ends of marriage, are directed to disposing the spouses to cooperate valiantly with the love of the Creator and Saviour, who through them will increase and enrich his family from day to day."

Catechism of the Catholic Church

	Sacred	Permanent	Exclusive	To have Children
Roman Catholic				
Presbyterian				
Methodist				
Church of Ireland				

MARRIAGE STATISTICS IN THE UNITED KINGDOM

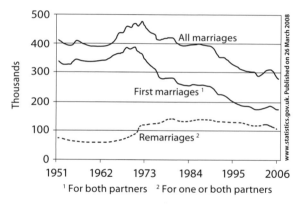

www.statistics.gov.uk. Published on 26 March 2008

[1] For both partners   [2] For one or both partners

The **Marriage Act 1836** and the **Registration Act 1836** came into force in 1837 in England and Wales and provided the statutory basis for regulating and recording marriages. The Marriage (Northern Ireland) Order 2003 provided a greater choice of marriage venues and types of ceremony available and made the preliminaries to a marriage the same for everyone.

IN A GROUP

Look at the graph showing the statistics and discuss the following:

1. In 2006, there were 275,140 weddings in the UK, a fall of 4% since 2005. Why do you think there was a 4% fall?

2. Marriages in England and Wales fell by 4% in 2006, whilst in Northern Ireland marriages increased 1%. Why do you think the statistics are different in Northern Ireland?

3. The long-term picture for UK weddings is one of decline from a peak of 480,285 marriages in 1972. Christians believe that marriage should be encouraged. What do you think could be done to encourage people to get married?

4. Since 1992, there have been more civil ceremonies in England and Wales than religious ceremonies. Why do you think more people are opting for a civil ceremony rather than a church wedding?

FURTHER THINKING

A 'sham marriage' is a marriage that is motivated by a desire for personal convenience rather than by love. For example, a sham marriage may take place to allow a person to live in a country of which he or she is not a citizen. The couple know the only purpose of the marriage is to obtain legal status for the man or woman to live in the country. A change in the law from 1 February 2005 was designed to discourage 'sham marriages' which may have been one of the many factors that have contributed to a drop in the number of marriages since 2004. Find out the details of this law.

WHY DO PEOPLE GET MARRIED?

You might think that people get married simply because they fall in love and want to be together forever! But people get married for a number of reasons. Look at the comments below. Draw two columns on a page. Put into one column the reasons you think are good and into the other column the reasons you think are bad.

John
"People marry to get company that they wouldn't get if they were single. That's why I got married. Nobody wants to return to an empty home, which is what happens if you don't marry."

Sarah
"I got married to show that I was completely committed to my boyfriend. I wanted the world to know that he was mine. And to let other women know that he is off-limits."

Andrew
"I just wanted everyone to know that I was in love…no seriously, I'd met the right girl. I'm 34 and have had a lot of girlfriends. But this time I knew I was ready to settle. Dawn is 29."

Michael
"We got married because we have three children. They were starting to get bullied at school for having a different surname to me. I just wanted them to be happy."

Anne
"I got married because I wanted to be financially secure. My husband is quite rich and if anything happened to him and we weren't married, all his money would have gone to his mother. I don't think so!"

Dave
"There is no way my mother would have let me live with Jane. It was just easier to get married. And, of course mother insisted on a church wedding. Marriage was the only way me and Jane could be together."

Annette
"We got married because I'm a Christian and I don't believe in sex before marriage. My husband agrees with me. We got married at 19 and have four children. I'm 25 now."

Donna
"I have to admit that I had always dreamed of a wedding day since I was little. It's not the only reason why I got married, of course, but we had a great day and wouldn't change a thing."

Trevor
"To get away from home. Pure and simple. My mother was driving me mad. Always interfering. At least now I've got someone to look after me who won't wreck my head!"

FOR YOUR FOLDER

1. State one reason why people get married.

2. Explain what Christians believe about the purpose of marriage.

 3. Name one of the vows taken by a couple in a church wedding service.

 4. Why do couples often exchange rings during a wedding ceremony?

5. What document must a couple sign after the wedding service to make them legally married?

6. Do you think people with little or no Christian faith should be allowed to get married in a church?

7. "Biblical teaching on marriage is not important in the twenty-first century. All that matters is that a couple wants to be together." Do you agree or disagree?

WHAT PROBLEMS DO MARRIAGES FACE?

Marriage is not always easy and many couples face problems which can put pressure on their relationship. You probably know of couples that are separated or divorced. In Northern Ireland it is estimated that one in three marriages end in separation or divorce. There were 2,362 divorces in 2007.

It is hard to pinpoint exactly why a marriage fails. Often it is a combination of a lot of things. However, some of the common pressures on marriage include:

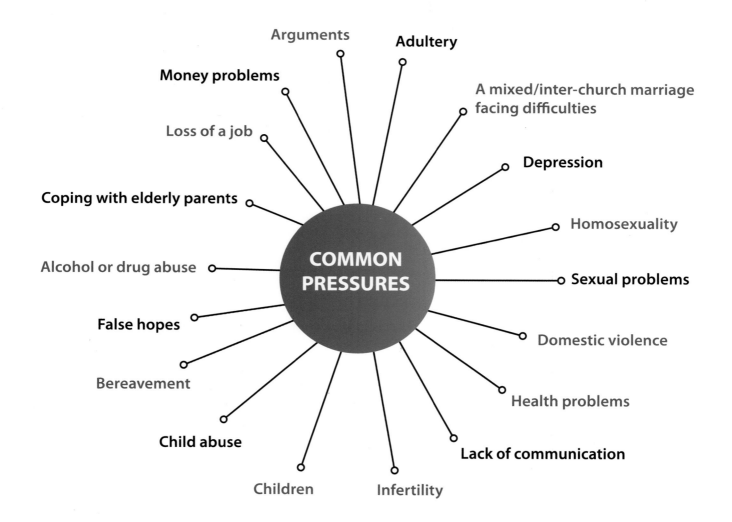

- Arguments
- Adultery
- Money problems
- A mixed/inter-church marriage facing difficulties
- Loss of a job
- Depression
- Coping with elderly parents
- Homosexuality
- Alcohol or drug abuse
- Sexual problems
- False hopes
- Domestic violence
- Bereavement
- Health problems
- Child abuse
- Lack of communication
- Children
- Infertility

COMMON PRESSURES

IN A GROUP

Choose three of these reasons. Discuss how each can put a strain on a marriage. Report back to the rest of the class.

In some circumstances one partner has sole responsibility for ending a marriage. For example, in the case of adultery one person may decide to leave their partner for someone else. However, often it is hard to identify who is guilty and who is innocent.

HOW CAN A TROUBLED MARRIAGE BE SAVED?

Most people would agree that it is probably best to try to sort out problems as they arise. But sometimes it is easier to ignore difficulties and say nothing rather than face up to things going wrong. Christians believe that it is important to avoid a separation and so a couple should try as hard as possible to make the relationship work. All the churches agree that counseling is vital when it comes to saving a troubled marriage. The Church of Ireland comments:

"Marriage can be challenging and especially so when we have huge demands on our time and emotional energy. Couples can drift apart and leave it too late to recover what has been lost and sometimes they are reluctant to share their difficulties. Perhaps they can't get a timely appointment at a Marriage Guidance organisation or perhaps, for whatever reason, they may prefer to seek help from someone from a church background" (The Church of Ireland Marriage Council).

MARRIAGE GUIDANCE AND COUNSELLING SERVICES

A number of organisations exist to help couples who experience difficulties in their marriage. Two of them are Relate and Accord.

relate
the relationship people

This is how Relate explains its services:
"Relate Northern Ireland is a registered charity, part of Relate, a federated charity which is the largest provider of relationship counselling and sex therapy in England, Wales and Northern Ireland. It works in partnership with the Department of Health and Social Services and Public Safety for Northern Ireland; the five Health and Social Care Trusts and also works in close cooperation with various charities, churches and community groups.

Relate Northern Ireland offers a range of relationship services that can help with a wide range of relationship issues such as: poor communication, rows, affairs, domestic violence and abuse, stress, anxiety, separation and divorce, impact of separation and divorce on children, second relationships and maintaining good relationships. The services are confidential and are available to, young people, families, couples and individuals irrespective of social class, religion, gender, ability, colour, creed, ethnicity or sexual orientation. The services include: relationship/family counselling, sex therapy, domestic violence and abuse counselling, life skills training and general support with relationship issues.

All sorts of people from a wide range of cultural and religious backgrounds benefit from Relate's services – married, cohabiting, single, young, old, same sex couples and family groups. They find that it helps them to understand difficulties in their relationships and to change things for the better, or to prevent small problems becoming bigger by talking about them. Client evaluations show that over 90% of clients rate the service provided as very good or good; more that 70% indicate that they wish they had come sooner.

Relate NI counsellors are highly trained in relationship issues to help people through all stages of their relationships:

- Single – contented or frustrated

- Loving someone – happiness and joy or agony
- To marry or not to marry? – one wants to, the other does not
- Married – contented or ...... and growing apart
- First baby – wonderful, but tiredness and emotional turmoil lead to misunderstandings and different sexual needs
- Family – demands, relatives
- Life changes – employment, finances, health, hobbies, bereavement
- Empty nest – children leaving home
- Separation/divorce – thinking it through

Counselling can help by enabling the couple, family or individual to consider what the difficulties are, how they arose and how to deal with them, with the assistance of an experienced and well trained counsellor."

> Find out the different ways in which Relate can help people facing relationship problems by looking up their website: www.relate.org.uk or www.relateni.org Some of the services you can research are:
>
> - Relationship counselling
> - Family counselling
> - Separation and divorce counselling
> - Psycho-sexual therapy
> - Young people's counselling
> - Listening ear service
> - Life skills courses
> - Pre-marriage or long term commitment course

ACCORD, Catholic Marriage Counselling Service is a Christian organisation based on Catholic principles. It offers a safe, professional and confidential process to help couples and individuals to explore, reflect upon and resolve difficulties in their marriage and relationship.

Counselling is arranged by contacting any one of ACCORD's centres throughout Ireland. ACCORD's counsellors deliver professional expertise in a reassuring atmosphere. They help to clarify a couple's particular situation, enabling them to express their thoughts and feelings and helping them to explore new options and agree a course of action.

> ### Did you know?
>
> 70% of people who attend counselling have children under the age of 11.
>
> Reduction in stress in ACCORD clients is significantly higher than other family support interventions in Ireland.
>
> 73% of people felt that they had gained great understanding of themselves.
>
> 54% of people spend up to six months thinking about coming to counselling, the remaining (46%) take longer.
>
> 92% of clients thought they would return to counselling if they had further relationship problems.
>
> ACCORD NI, www.accordni.com, date accessed 2 April 2009

IN A GROUP

> Relate is not directly linked to any church or denomination, although it works in close cooperation with various charities, churches and community groups. Do you think their advice would differ in any way from that of a church based counselling service such as ACCORD?

DIVORCE

In many cases, despite attempts at trying to stay together, some couples admit that the only way forward for them is to get divorced. The Matrimonial Causes (Northern Ireland) Order 1978 states that to get a divorce a person has to satisfy the courts that the marriage has irretrievably broken down and that one of the following grounds exist:

- Adultery – by the other party

- Behaviour – which has made it unreasonable for the couple to stay together

- Desertion – for two years

- Separation and consent – the parties have lived apart for two years, and the other party consents to the divorce

- Five year separation – the parties have lived apart for five years

WHO IS AFFECTED BY DIVORCE?

HUSBAND CUTS HOUSE IN TWO

A Cambodian husband who separated from his wife after 40 years cut their house in two. He and friends moved his belongings to one side of the house then sawed and chiselled it off. The man moved his part of the house to his parent's property to live in it there, while the wife continues to reside in her precariously perched upright half.

Divorce can be a stressful time and can cause people to act in unreasonable ways. Getting a divorce is not an easy decision to make because it will affect more than just the couple themselves. More often that not, the children and grandparents are the bigger losers when a couple decides to split up.

Children of divorced parents can suffer in the following ways:

- **Confusion** over who to be loyal to – a child might feel torn between his or her two parents.

- **Grief** – a child will have to live with one parent. The child will lose out on day-to-day contact with the other parent and may experience feelings of loss and sadness, similar to those experienced when suffering bereavement.

- **Behaviour** – a child may be very angry over what has happened. He or she may start to misbehave at school; may suffer from eating disorders, or in the case of a young child, suffer from bed-wetting. All of these are symptoms of stress.

The Catholic Church comments:

> "Divorce is immoral also because it introduces disorder into the family and into society. This disorder brings grave harm to the deserted spouse, to children traumatised by the separation of their parents and often torn between them, and because of its contagious effect which makes it truly a plague on society".

Catechism of the Catholic Church

Just as the children suffer, the parents themselves may also find it hard to adjust to the new lifestyle:

- Fear over what lies ahead
- Worry about money
- Loneliness
- Stress of looking after the children on their own
- Lack of support from in-laws who may be quick to blame
- Depression

WHAT THE BIBLE SAYS ABOUT DIVORCE

According to the Bible, God's plan is for marriage to be a lifelong and permanent commitment:

> *"So they are no longer two, but one. Therefore what God has joined together, let man not separate."*

Matthew 19:6

The Old Testament prophet Malachi clearly declares God's opinion of divorce:

> *"'I hate divorce,' says the Lord God of Israel."*

Malachi 2:16

However, some Christians believe that God knows that since a marriage involves two sinful human beings, divorce is going to happen. The Old Testament book of Deuteronomy says that God laid down some laws in order to protect the rights of divorcees, especially women (Deuteronomy 24:1–4). Jesus pointed out that these laws were given because of the hardness of people's hearts, not because they were what God wanted (Matthew 19:8).

The debate over whether the Bible allows divorce and remarriage centres on Jesus' words in Matthew 5:31–32:

> *"It was also said, 'Anyone who divorces his wife must give her a written notice of divorce.' But now I tell you: if anyone divorces his wife, for any cause other than her unfaithfulness, then he is guilty of making her commit adultery if she marries again; and the man who marries her commits adultery also."*

The phrase "other than her unfaithfulness" is the only condition for divorce. Jesus seems to be saying that divorce is allowed if sexual immorality is committed. Sexual relations are such a special part of the marital bond, *"the two will become one flesh"* (Genesis 2:24; Matthew 19:5; Ephesians 5:31), that breaking that bond by sexual relations outside of marriage is a reason for divorce. Some Christians, although not all, argue that Jesus also has remarriage in mind in this passage.

Some Christians also believe that Paul's words in 1 Corinthians 7:15 allow remarriage if an unbelieving spouse divorces a believer.

However, remarriage is not mentioned here. It says only that a believer is not bound to continue a marriage if an unbelieving spouse wants to leave. Others claim that abuse (of spouse or child) is a valid reason for divorce even though this is not mentioned in the Bible as a reason.

One church marriage guidance counsellor comments:

> "Sometimes lost in the debate about divorce is the fact that unfaithfulness is an allowance for divorce, not a requirement for divorce. Even if adultery has been committed a couple can, through God's grace, learn to forgive and begin to rebuild their marriage. Surely we can follow God's example (Ephesians 4:32) and even forgive the sin of adultery?"

WHAT THE CHURCHES SAY ABOUT DIVORCE

Most churches teach that divorce is to be seen only as a last resort after every possible effort toward reconciliation has failed. Just as the Bible advises couples to enter into marriage carefully, so divorce should be avoided at all costs. Christians believe that honouring and upholding the marriage vows brings glory to God.

The Presbyterian Church, Methodist Church and the Church of Ireland all accept civil divorce as an end to marriage. They allow the remarriage of divorced people in church, but only if the minister is willing to perform the ceremony. A minister can refuse on the grounds of his own conscience.

The Roman Catholic Church does not allow divorce: "Adultery, divorce, polygamy, and free union are grave offenses against the dignity of marriage" (*Catechism of the Catholic Church*). Marriage is regarded as a sacrament and as such cannot be dissolved or ended. Even if a civil divorce is granted to a couple, the Church still believes that in the eyes of God they are still married and are not allowed to remarry:

> "If a husband, separated from his wife, approaches another woman, he is an adulterer because he makes that woman commit adultery, and the woman who lives with him is an adulteress, because she has drawn another's husband to herself".

> St Basil, *Moralia 73*, 1: PG 31, 849–852, taken from *Catechism of the Catholic Church*

However, the Catholic Church does acknowledge that marriages can run into difficulties:

> "Yet there are some situations in which living together becomes practically impossible for a variety of reasons. In such cases the Church permits the physical separation of the couple and their living apart. The spouses do not cease to be husband and wife before God and so are not free to contract a new union. In this difficult situation, the best solution would be, if possible, reconciliation. The Christian community is called to help these persons live out their situation in a Christian manner and in fidelity to their marriage bond which remains indissoluble."

> *Familiaris Consortio 84*, taken from *Catechism of the Catholic Church*

Many Catholic Christians argue that the church needs to move with the times. Years ago problems such as domestic violence, abuse and even adultery were more likely to be kept secret. People often put on a brave face and pretended that everything was fine, to prevent bringing shame on the family. Nowadays people no longer feel that they have to suffer in silence. Some Christians argue that with the evidence that they have, the church should allow divorce in serious circumstances. What do you think?

FOR YOUR FOLDER

1. What is divorce?
2. Explain why some Christians do not agree with divorce.
3. Explain why some marriages run into trouble.
4. Name an organisation that helps couples who are experiencing marriage difficulties.
5. What can the church do to help couples who feel that divorce is their only option?
6. Do you think a marriage between two people with a strong Christian faith is more likely to succeed than that of a couple with no religious faith?
7. Do you think that church ministers who get divorced should lose their jobs?
8. "Today's more relaxed attitude to divorce has damaged the whole of society." Do you agree or disagree?

Chapter 2

MATTERS OF LIFE AND DEATH

● ABORTION

Abortion is the act of deliberately ending a pregnancy before normal childbirth, killing the foetus in the process. It is a very sensitive and painful issue for those facing the problem of an unwanted pregnancy. The issue of abortion continues to be a hot topic for debate. There are a variety of opinions about whether it is the right or wrong thing to do.

WHY IS ABORTION A CONTROVERSIAL ISSUE?

The debate about abortion is so controversial because there are disagreements in philosophy, medicine and theology about when a foetus (a baby in the womb before it is fully formed) becomes sufficiently human to have the right to life. People hold a variety of opinions with some at one extreme believing that the embryo must be treated as a person 'from conception' (see the *Catechism of the Catholic Church*), to others taking the view that life begins at the stage when the 'foetus can survive outside the womb'. (This is the most common criterion used by governments in drafting laws regulating abortion. It is known as **viability**).

IN A GROUP

WHAT DO YOU BELIEVE?
Research the stages of development of the foetus. Your biology teacher might be able to help you with this. Discuss when you think the foetus becomes human:
- Conception
- Implantation
- 'Quickening'
- Brain activity
- Viability of the foetus
- Birth

A DIFFICULT QUESTION:

"Is abortion morally wrong?" This is one of the main questions asked by people today. The answer is not straightforward and may depend upon the circumstances. For example, one person may answer this question by saying:

> "No, abortion is not morally wrong, but there may be cases where abortion is not the best way forward."

Another person might say:

> "Yes, abortion is morally wrong, but maybe having an abortion would be better than the alternative."

IN A GROUP

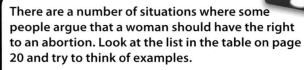

There are a number of situations where some people argue that a woman should have the right to an abortion. Look at the list in the table on page 20 and try to think of examples.

If you don't know, ask your parents or your teacher to help you.

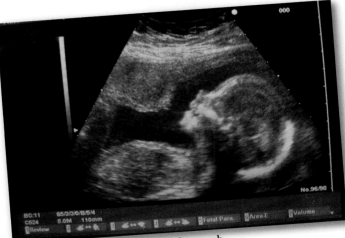
An ultrasound scan of a baby in the womb.

How the woman could be affected by an unwanted pregnancy	Examples of a special case
Damage to mental health	
Damage to physical health	
Damage to family life	Cases where the child will suffer from some severe mental or physical abnormality.
Damage to career prospects	
Damage to financial prospects	
Damage to plans for her life	

SOCIAL VIEWPOINTS

Most people today have some sort of opinion on abortion but unless the issue affects them directly, they may not give it much thought. However, there are two main groups of people who take a strong stance on the abortion issue and devote time and energy to their cause. They stand at two extremes and are known as **pro-life** and **pro-choice** groups.

PRO-LIFE GROUPS

Pro-life groups argue that intentionally-caused abortion is always wrong. They believe that the foetus is an innocent and defenceless being that needs to be protected. There are a number of pro-life groups: the Society for the Protection of Unborn Children (SPUC), LIFE and Precious Life. These groups try to educate ordinary people, politicians and governments about how abortion is the wrong path to take. They also provide support for women and children.

WHAT ARE THE ARGUMENTS AGAINST ABORTION?

1. All human life is of equal value, even a foetus or an embryo.

2. The foetus has the right to life because it is a potential human being from the moment the egg is fertilised.

3. A foetus is not the same sort of thing as a leg or a kidney: it is not just a part of a woman's body, but is (to some extent) a separate person with its own right to life.

4. A foetus is an innocent human being and killing an innocent human being is wrong. Abortion is the deliberate killing of a foetus.

5. Abortion is contrary to the medical ethics in the Hippocratic Oath which states, "I will maintain the utmost respect for human life, from the time of conception."

KEYWORD

THE HIPPOCRATIC OATH
A promise traditionally made by new doctors to treat all people fairly, and to seek to preserve life. It is named after an ancient Greek physician.

6. Abortion can damage the long-term physical and emotional health of women.

7. People should take responsibility for the consequences of their actions. When a woman has sex she takes the risk of bringing a foetus into existence and has a duty of care to the foetus.

8. People do not have the complete right to control their bodies. For example, there are laws against euthanasia. The same should apply to abortion.

9. If there is disability, social problems or difficult circumstances surrounding the child's conception, the right response is one of compassion for the parents and the child. It can never be compassionate to deliberately take innocent human life.

10. If women were not able to have abortions so easily, governments would be forced to invest more money in supporting mothers. Women could be given what they need to survive financially and socially as mothers, such as affordable childcare and flexible working hours.

11. Many women are unable to have children. It is better to have the child adopted than to kill the unborn foetus.

SPECIAL CASE: DISABILITY IN THE FOETUS

In our society there are laws protecting people with disability. For example, people with disabilities should not be discriminated against, and society should do everything possible to allow disabled people to play a full part in ordinary life. However, under the 1967 Abortion Act (UK) termination of a pregnancy was allowed at any time if there was a significant risk of the baby being born seriously disabled. This was severely criticised by the Disability Rights Commission as being offensive to disabled people and suggesting that their lives are not as important as the lives of the rest of people. What do you think? Look at the following statements and give your opinion:

- Allowing disability as a reason for abortion implies that disabled people are not as worthwhile as the rest of people in society.
- This is offensive to disabled people and will make them feel less valued.

PRO-CHOICE GROUPS

Pro-choice groups argue that intentional abortion is acceptable. Abortion Rights, the national pro-choice campaign, was formed in 2003 by the merger of the two long standing and influential campaigns: the National Abortion Campaign (NAC) and the Abortion Law Reform Association (ALRA). They seek to build support for a woman's right to choose and encourage individuals and organisations to get involved.

WHAT ARE THE ARGUMENTS FOR ABORTION?

1. An embryo is a cluster of cells and not an actual human being.

2. The woman should be regarded as a person and not just as a container for the foetus.

3. Women need the right to abortion in order to have full rights over their own bodies, including the right to decide whether or not to carry a foetus to birth. Without this right they do not have the same moral status as men.

4. Banning abortion puts women at risk by forcing them to use illegal and back-street abortionists.

5. Women need free access to abortion in order to achieve full social, political and economic equality with men.

6. A woman may not be able to cope with the birth of a child if she has been raped, or is too young, or is mentally incapable of continuing the pregnancy.

7. People should take responsibility for the consequences of their actions. Abortion is a responsible way of dealing with an unwanted child.

POLITICAL VIEWPOINTS

In some countries, for example Ireland, abortion is illegal, while in others it is allowed in special cases. In England, Scotland and Wales abortion is allowed if certain conditions are met. These conditions are set out in the **Abortion Act 1967** and **Human Fertilisation and Embryology Act 1990**. Abortion is allowed if two other doctors agree:

> "that the continuance of the pregnancy would involve risk to the life of the pregnant woman, or of injury to the physical or mental health of the pregnant woman or any existing children of her family, greater than if the pregnancy were terminated."

or

> "that there is a substantial risk that if the child were born it would suffer from such physical or mental abnormalities as to be seriously handicapped."

What does this mean in ordinary language? The following list helps to explain the circumstances where abortion is allowed:

1. If continuing the pregnancy is a risk to the life of the mother (abortion allowed until birth).

2. If there is a risk that the mother may suffer mentally or physically if the pregnancy is

allowed to continue (abortion allowed up until 24 weeks of the pregnancy*). For example, mentally the mother may be unable to cope with a child or may be too young to cope with a child. Or the pregnancy may be too distressing if it is the result of a crime, for example, rape.

3. If continuing the pregnancy is a risk to the physical or mental health of any existing children of the pregnant woman (abortion allowed up until 24 weeks of the pregnancy).

4. If there is a risk that once the child was born it would have serious physical handicaps or mental defects.

*Countries that allow abortion lay down a maximum age after which the foetus must not be aborted, regardless of the circumstances.

IN A GROUP

Which of these reasons would be more acceptable to opponents of abortion?

NORTHERN IRELAND AND ABORTION

In Northern Ireland abortion can be obtained only if the woman's life is at risk and in some cases of foetal abnormality. Many people are frustrated by the situation in Northern Ireland and argue that it is out of step with the rest of the UK. As a result many women travel to England to obtain abortions. It has been suggested that this defeats the purpose of the ban on abortion in NI, as women who want one can avail of services elsewhere in the UK. New guidelines were published by the Department of Health on 20 March 2009, providing Northern Ireland health professionals with guidance on terminating pregnancies. Some members of the Family Planning Association have seen this publication as the first step towards governmental recognition of women's right to abortion in certain situations within Northern Ireland.

Debate in the House of Commons, 2008

In 2008 there was a debate in the House of Commons on lowering the time limit for abortion as part of the consideration of the Human Fertilisation and Embryology Bill. MPs voted on a series of abortion limits of 12, 16, 20 and 22 weeks – all of which were rejected. This was the first major challenge to Britain's abortion laws since 1990, when the legal limit was lowered from 28 to 24 weeks.

Conservative leader David Cameron voted for a 20 week limit and then for a cut to a 22 week limit. Prime Minister Gordon Brown and most of the cabinet voted to keep the existing 24 week limit, as did Nick Clegg, the Liberal Democrat leader. But Catholic cabinet ministers Ruth Kelly, Des Browne and Paul Murphy voted for the lowest option – 12 weeks. A bid to cut the limit to 12 weeks was opposed by 393 votes to 71. A further attempt to get the limit down to 16 weeks was defeated by 387 votes to 84.

As a result of the voting, the time limit for abortion was kept at 24 weeks.

IN A GROUP

"In modern Britain the most dangerous place to be is in your mother's womb. It should be a place of sanctity".

Edward Leigh, Conservative MP

Do you agree or disagree?
Give reasons for your answer

ABORTION STATISTICS

In 2007, for women resident in England and Wales the total number of abortions were 198,500 – a rise of 2.5% from 2006. The total number of abortions for non-residents carried out in hospitals and clinics in England and Wales were 7,100. For more up-to-date figures refer to the Department of Health Publications at:
www.dh.gov.uk/en/Publicationsandstatistics

BIBLICAL AND CHURCH VIEWPOINTS

Abortion is not a modern issue. It has been used in the past to get rid of unwanted children. Even before the time of Jesus in Greek and Roman society abortion was commonplace. There is evidence to suggest that protection of the unborn was not a priority and that abortion was accepted. Several philosophers, such as Plato and Aristotle supported abortion. Aristotle believed that female embryos developed more slowly than male embryos, and that the life of a male foetus did not begin until 40 days after conception, whereas the life of a female foetus began 80 days after conception!

The *Oath of Hippocrates* (460–357 BC) shows that not everyone in ancient society agreed with abortion. Part of the oath addresses the issue directly:

"…Neither will I administer a poison to anybody when asked to do so, nor will I suggest such a course. Similarly, I will not give to a woman a pessary to cause abortion."

Hippocrates, (English translation) Jones, WHS, London, 1972, Vol 1, p 229

While there are no Jewish texts that specifically condemn abortion, emphasis is placed on the importance of early life in the womb. With the emergence of Christianity the belief that all life is sacred continued to grow, although there is no reference to abortion in the New Testament. However, the *Epistle of Barnabas*, a writing of the first century, comments that:

"Thou shalt not slay the child by procuring abortion; nor, again; shalt thou destroy it after it is born."

The Epistle of Barnabas, Grand Rapids, 1971

Tertullian, a great Christian writer in the early church, also condemned abortion, scolding not only the woman but those who assist her. He believed a foetus received its soul at the moment of conception.

The first Christian council to address the issue of abortion was the Council of Elvira in Spain in the fourth century. At this meeting 81 canons (religious laws) were produced, one of which stated:

"If a woman conceives in adultery and then has an abortion, she may not commune again, even as death approaches, because she has sinned twice."

In other words, the woman was excommunicated (made to leave the church). Other councils followed with similar decrees. However, as time passed the focus shifted from concern for the soul of the woman to concern for the foetus itself.

WHAT THE BIBLE SAYS ABOUT ABORTION

In general the Bible does not have much to say about abortion. There is one Bible passage (Exodus 21:22) which relates to miscarriage not abortion. However, it is relevant in discussing the importance of the foetus. In this passage the law said that if a person causes a miscarriage they had to pay "*a fine*"

to the husband of the woman. If they also caused the death of the woman, *"then they could be killed"*. There has been a lot of debate over the meaning of this passage. Some people argue that it is saying that the foetus is not as important to God as a grown person because of the differences in punishment. Others disagree and say the fact that a punishment is given at all shows that the foetus is as important to God as a person.

Christians point to other references in the Bible to argue that the unborn child is a person and should be treated as such. Look up the references in the table below and explain how they support this view. The first one has been completed for you.

VIEW THAT THE UNBORN CHILD IS EQUAL TO A LIVING PERSON		
Reference	**Copy out the verse(s)**	**How does this support the view?**
Genesis 1:27	"So God created human beings, making them to be like himself"	The Bible teaches that all life is sacred, created by God. This includes the life of the unborn.
Psalm 22:9		
Psalm 139:13 –16		
Isaiah 44:2		
Jeremiah 1:5		
Luke 1:41, 44		
Luke 18:16		
Galatians 1:15		

WHAT THE CHURCHES SAY ABOUT ABORTION

The Christian churches all agree that life begins in the womb. However, they do differ on whether or not abortion is acceptable. Look at the following church statements and summarise the viewpoint of each of the Christian denominations represented:

CHRISTIAN DENOMINATION	DISCUSSION ON ABORTION
Roman Catholic	"The direct and voluntary killing of an innocent human being is always gravely immoral". "Life must be respected with the utmost care from the moment of conception. Abortion and infanticide are abominable crimes." *Gaudium et Spes*, 51:3
Presbyterian Church	"The scriptures leave us in no doubt that from his earliest days in the womb, the unborn child is fully human, a person made in the image of God" *Leaflet on Abortion*, p1
Anglican Church (Church of Ireland/Church of England)	The Lambeth conference of 1958 received a Committee Report in which it was stated: "In the strongest terms, Christians reject the practice of induced abortion, or infanticide, which involves the killing of a life already conceived (as well as a violation of the personality of the mother) save at the dictate of strict and undeniable medical necessity." Statement from the Church of Ireland Standing Committee for the General Synod 1982, to the Taoiseach, Mr Haughey: "We cannot emphasis too strongly the right to life and this includes the right of the yet unborn." In March 1998 a working group was asked by the Role of the Church Committee to draft a submission to the Interdepartmental Working Group on Abortion, Department of Health and Children of the Government of the Republic of Ireland: "We are very concerned about women facing crisis pregnancies and as a church we endeavour to offer compassion and love to them in their anxieties…The deliberate termination of an intra uterine life cannot be right but many in our church believe that exceptional cases may arise which mean that abortion ought to be an option and may even be a necessity in a few very rare cases. No abortion is ever desirable – at most it can only be described as the lesser of two evils, and always undertaken with a profound sense of sadness and regret…The availability of abortion in Great Britain is a reality and with sadness we recognise that thousands of women from both North and South make use of that facility each year. On their return to Ireland they do not need our condemnation to make their situation worse – instead our church must offer them spiritual, emotional and practical support as they rebuild their lives." * * The text was subsequently approved by the Role of the Church Committee and submitted to the Interdepartmental Working Group with the approval of the Standing Committee of the Church of Ireland. Its contents are produced by the Medical Ethics Working Group as a contribution to discussion of issues in Ireland. As such they have only the authority of that group and are not intended to reflect the policy of the Role of the Church Committee or of any other Church of Ireland body.

Methodist	From *The Status of the Unborn*, a report received by the Methodist Conference 1992: "The worth of the human race itself hinges on reverence for human life at every stage and the long tradition of Christian teaching is marked by an abhorrence of destroying the life in the womb. But a right to life does not mean an absolute right. Other lives have impinging rights. The life of the mother, whose survival may be crucial because care for the existing family heavily depend upon her, would appear to have priority over that of the foetus, if a choice has to be made…As a Church we are in favour of allowing the parties concerned to have the pregnancy terminated in the following cases: when there is grave risk to the mother's physical and mental health; when the pregnancy was the result of rape; when there is gross abnormality of the foetus."

WHAT OTHER RELIGIONS SAY ABOUT ABORTION

All the major world religions take strong positions on abortion and regard it as a serious issue. Those involved in an abortion can be affected spiritually, as well as emotionally. They often turn to their faith for comfort and guidance before making any decisions or to search for a way to deal with guilt after having an abortion.

ISLAM AND ABORTION

The Qur'an does not explicitly refer to abortion but gives guidance on related matters which can be applied to abortion. Muslims place great value on the sanctity of life. The Qur'an states: "Whosoever has killed a soul, it is as though he has murdered all of mankind". So most Muslim scholars would say that a foetus in the womb is protected by Islam as a human life.

However, many Muslims accept that abortion may be allowed in certain cases, for example, to save the life of the mother which is regarded as the "lesser of two evils".

Different schools of Muslim law hold different views as to when an abortion can be carried out. Some schools of thought allow abortion in the first 16 weeks of pregnancy, while others only permit it in the first seven weeks. It is rarely allowed after 120 days of pregnancy, although all schools of Muslim law accept that abortion is allowed after 120 days if continuing the pregnancy would put the mother's life in real danger.

JUDAISM AND ABORTION

In Judaism a foetus is not considered to be a person until it is born. Before birth it is considered to be a part of the mother's body, although it does possess certain characteristics of a person and as such should be protected. For example, Jewish law allows desecration of the Sabbath in order to save the life of a foetus.

Abortion is not explicitly referred to in the Hebrew Bible (Old Testament). However, Judaism places great emphasis on the sanctity of human life: "Whoever destroys one life is as if he destroyed a whole world, and whoever preserves a life is as if he preserved the whole world."

Mishnah

Judaism does not forbid abortion, but it does not allow abortion on demand. Abortion is allowed in extreme cases. For example, Judaism teaches that the mother's life takes precedence over the life of the foetus therefore Jewish law insists on an abortion if it will save the mother's life.

FURTHER THINKING

1. **Abortion and religion**
Research: choose one of the following religions and find out what it says about abortion:

   • Buddhism

   • Hinduism

   • Sikhism

2. **Abortion and gender selection**
In some countries, for example India and China, parents prefer to have boy babies. A termination can be carried out because the foetus is female. There is a major problem with deliberately aborting foetuses that would be born as girls. Find out what you can about abortion in these countries and report your findings to the rest of the class.

FOR YOUR FOLDER

SP09

1. What is abortion?

2. Give some reasons for the rise in the number of abortions in our society.

3. Explain why abortion is such a controversial issue.

4. Describe one situation when a Christian might agree with a woman's right to choose abortion.

SP09

5. Why might a Christian advise a teenager to put her child up for adoption rather than have an abortion?

6. Why do most Christians argue that the foetus is a real person?

7. How do the different Christian denominations view abortion?

SP09

8. "Christians should accept that sometimes abortion is necessary." Do you agree or disagree?

IN A GROUP

In discussing the rights and wrongs of abortion, arguments tend to focus on the rights of the foetus or the mother. The rights of the father are rarely taken into consideration. What happens if the father wants the baby but the mother wants to have an abortion? Or what about the case where the father wants the mother to have an abortion but she wants the pregnancy to continue?

Discuss the following: Do you think that it is right for a woman to legally deprive a man of his right to become a father?

FURTHER THINKING

Find out about the Roe v Wade abortion case in the USA.

● EUTHANASIA

The word euthanasia comes from the Greek language and means 'good death'. Very often people call euthanasia 'mercy killing', perhaps thinking of someone who is terminally ill and suffering prolonged, unbearable pain.

Euthanasia can be carried out either by doing something, such as giving a lethal injection, or by ceasing to do something necessary to keep the person alive, such as stopping the use of a feeding tube.

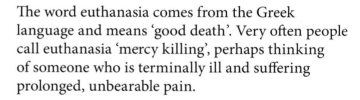

EUTHANASIA: KEY TERMS	
Active euthanasia	A person directly and deliberately causes the patient's death, for example, by an overdose of pain-killers.
Passive euthanasia	A person does not directly take the patient's life; they just allow them to die. This can be by withdrawing or withholding treatment.
Voluntary euthanasia	Euthanasia is carried out at the request of the person who dies.
Non-voluntary euthanasia	The person is unconscious or otherwise unable (for example, a very young baby or a person of extremely low intelligence) to make a meaningful choice between living and dying, and someone makes the decision on their behalf.
Involuntary euthanasia	The person who dies wants to live but is killed anyway. It is usually the same as murder.
Palliative care	Medical, emotional or spiritual care given to a person who is terminally ill and which is aimed at reducing suffering rather than curing.
Living wills	A living will is a document that sets out a patient's wishes regarding how they want to be treated if they become seriously ill and unable to make or communicate their own choices. It is not an instrument of euthanasia, but a request to doctors in advance, not to give certain medical treatments.

VOLUNTARY EUTHANASIA

Voluntary euthanasia is supported by groups such as Dignity in Dying. It simply means that a person wants to die and wants help to do so. This can take many forms:

- Asking for direct help to die.
- Refusing medical treatment.
- Asking for medical treatment to be withdrawn, or life support machines to be switched off.
- Refusing food.

INVOLUNTARY EUTHANASIA

Involuntary euthanasia is not openly supported by any group in Britain or Ireland. It means that a person wants to live but is killed anyway. This is usually murder but not always.

Look at the following example:

A person is trapped in a burning house and is screaming for help. It is obvious that the home heating oil tank will catch fire, explode and spread the fire. The fire brigade is nowhere in sight. A passing hunter realises that the person will suffer an agonising death from burns. He shoots the person dead with his rifle.

IN A GROUP

Did the hunter do the right thing? Can you think of a similar scenario where a person may feel it is better to kill a person than leave them to suffer?

Difficult Questions:

Euthanasia is not a clear cut issue. There are a number of questions that are raised in the debate on euthanasia. Some of them are:

- Does an individual who has no hope of recovery have the right to decide how and when to end their life?

- Is it ever right for another person to end the life of a terminally ill patient who is in severe pain or enduring other suffering?

- If euthanasia is sometimes right, under what circumstances is it right?

- Is there any moral difference between killing someone and letting them die?

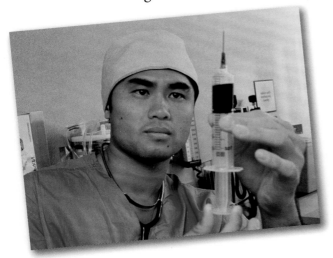

EUTHANASIA AND THE LAW

Euthanasia is illegal in Britain and in most countries. However, it is legal in the some countries such as Switzerland and the Netherlands. For most people, to kill another person deliberately is considered to be wrong, even if the other person asks you to kill them. It is also a criminal offence in the UK, punishable by 14 years imprisonment, to assist, aid or counsel somebody in relation to taking their own life.

Some people refer to euthanasia as 'assisted suicide', which simply means helping someone to kill him or herself. Several attempts to legalise assisted suicide in the UK have been rejected. The most recent, in 2006, was defeated in the House of Lords by 148 votes to 100. The following report explains what happened.

Assisted Dying Bill, May 2006

The House of Lords has blocked a bill that would allow terminally ill people to be helped to die. Lord Joffe's bill, which had its second reading on Friday 12 May 2006, proposed that after signing a legal declaration that they wanted to die, a patient's doctor could prescribe a lethal dose of medication that the patient could take themselves. Only people with less than six months to live, who are

suffering unbearably and deemed to be of sound mind and not depressed would be able to end their life.

Peers spent the day in a passionate debate on whether or not it was right to allow a person who was terminally ill to be given drugs they could then use to end their own life.

Lord Joffe argued: "We must find a solution to the unbearable suffering of patients whose needs cannot be met by palliative care."

The debate highlights divisions between supporters of the right to die and those who want better palliative care. Opponents of the bill urged for more to be done instead to improve palliative care for terminally ill patients.

The bill's supporters said doctors should be able to prescribe drugs so a terminally ill person suffering terrible pain could choose to end his or her life. These included Labour's Baroness David aged 92. She said:

"If I were terminally ill, I believe I would be the only person with the right to decide how I died, and whether I preferred palliative care to assisted dying. It would provide me with an additional option on how to end my life, which I would find tremendously reassuring."

Mark Slattery, of the charity Dignity in Dying, formerly the Voluntary Euthanasia Society, said the campaign to introduce an assisted dying bill would continue.

'Lords block Assisted Dying Bill', BBC News, 12 May 2006, www.bbc.co.uk, accessed 2 April 2009

Response to the Assisted Dying Bill

Britain's faith leaders joined forces to protest against Lord Joffe's proposals. In an open letter to both Houses of Parliament, the religious leaders condemned the bill, saying:

"Assisted suicide and euthanasia will radically change the social air we all breathe by severely undermining respect for life…We, the undersigned, hold all human life to be sacred and worthy of the utmost respect and note with concern that repeated attempts are being made to persuade Parliament to change the law on intentional killing so as to allow assisted suicide and voluntary euthanasia for those who are terminally ill."

'Assisted Dying Bill', Audio clip: Sunday programme discussion, 9 October 2005, BBC News, www.bbc.co.uk, accessed 2 April 2009

ARGUMENTS FOR EUTHANASIA

Those in favour of euthanasia argue that:

- many people think that a person has the right to control his or her life and should be able to determine at what time and in what way he or she will die.

- a civilised society should allow people to die in dignity and without pain.

- UK law already acknowledges that people have the right to die. The Suicide Act (UK) 1961 and the Criminal Justice Act (NI) 1966 made it legal for people to take their own lives.

Debbie Purdy's Story

Debbie Purdy, from Bradford, was diagnosed with primary progressive Multiple Sclerosis in March 1995. The 45 year old from Bradford has been confined to a wheelchair since 2001. You can read about Debbie on the website for the campaign group Dignity in Dying at www.dignityindying.org.uk

Debbie explains her worst fears:
"What worries me the most about my disease is that it is degenerative. It is incurable. It will keep on getting worse and it will not stop. I have to live with the uncertainty of what this may mean. It may mean I lose control of my arms, of my ability to speak, swallow or breathe."

If her pain becomes unbearable, Debbie wants to go to Switzerland where, unlike the UK, assisted suicide is legal. However, she is worried about her husband being prosecuted on his return for assisting. Under UK law, helping somebody die carries a sentence of up to 14 years.

Sarah Wootton, of Dignity in Dying, which supports Ms Purdy, said: "This case is about choice. Debbie should have the option to die at a time of her choosing should she feel her suffering has become unbearable."

However, Dr Peter Saunders, of Care Not Killing, www.carenotkilling.org.uk , points out: "It's not against the law to commit suicide – but assisting suicide is a crime. And it's a crime because a law allowing it could so easily be exploited or abused."

Debbie Purdy wanted to find out if her husband would be arrested for assisting her suicide, but in 2008 she lost her legal bid at the High Court to clarify the law on assisted suicide.

In 2000 **Diane Pretty**, who had motor neurone disease, petitioned the High Court, seeking a change in the law to allow her husband to help her end her life should she become too disabled to do so alone. This had an impact on Debbie. "It concentrated my mind, especially as she was only five years older than me," says Debbie. "And when she died two years later – in exactly the way she dreaded, choking to death – I realised that was my worst nightmare. It frightened me even more that Diane's express wishes had been ignored."

Several attempts to legalise assisted suicide in Britain have been rejected.
The most recent, in 2006 was defeated in the House of Lords by 148 votes to 100.

Information taken from BBC News, www.bbc.co.uk and *Telegraph*, www.telegraph.co.uk, accessed 2 April 2009

ARGUMENTS AGAINST EUTHANASIA

- Human life is sacred because it's a gift from God. Only God should decide when to end it.

- Accepting euthanasia suggests that some lives (those of the disabled or sick) are worth less than others. All human beings should be valued, irrespective of age, sex, race, religion, social status or their potential for achievement.

- If euthanasia was made legal, the laws regulating it would be abused, and people would be killed who didn't really want to die. Age Concern warned that the UK's elderly feared they were at risk of not being revived simply because of their age.

- Suffering may have a positive value.

- Proper palliative care makes euthanasia unnecessary.

- Vulnerable people – the elderly, lonely, sick or distressed – would feel pressure, whether real or imagined, to request an early death.

Jane Campbell's Story

Jane Campbell MBE, Chair of the Social Care Institute for Excellence from 2000 to 2006, is a Disability Rights commissioner and Not Dead Yet UK convener. She argues for the right to live:

"Assisted dying is not a simple question of increasing choice for those of us who live our lives close to death. It raises deep concerns about how we are viewed by society and by ourselves. I have a severe form of spinal muscular atrophy, and require 24-hour assistance. Many people who do not know me believe I would be 'better off dead'. Even more argue: 'I couldn't live like that.' And some suggest that advances in genetic screening should be used to enable parents to choose whether to have a child with disabilities."

"...I benefit from excellent medical care. I live in an adapted bungalow, and my local authority provides proper care support that enables me to choose my own personal assistants. I am not dependent on family and loved ones. I love my good life."

'Stop trying to kill us off', 9 May 2006, *The Guardian*, www.theguardian.co.uk, accessed 3 April 2009

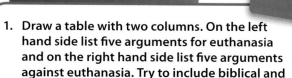

FOR YOUR FOLDER

1. Draw a table with two columns. On the left hand side list five arguments for euthanasia and on the right hand side list five arguments against euthanasia. Try to include biblical and church opinions as part of your answer.

2. Can you be neutral? During 2005 the British Medical Association dropped its historic opposition to euthanasia, adopting a neutral stance on the issue. What is meant by the term 'a neutral stance'? Do you think it is possible to be neutral about an issue like euthanasia?

PALLATIVE CARE

Palliative care is physical, emotional and spiritual care for a dying person when cure is impossible. It includes compassion and support for the patient, the family and friends. It gives the patient and their

family a chance to spend quality time together, with as much distress removed as possible. They can use this time to say their last goodbyes in a caring environment.

It has been suggested that competent palliative care could be enough to prevent a person feeling any need to contemplate euthanasia. Representatives of Britain's faith groups argue that providing good care does not require any change in the law but a reprioritisation of National Health Service resources, to make sure that centres of palliative care exist for those who need them.

Many people believe that a strong faith in God or a higher power can help the terminally ill face death. Christians look to the suffering of Christ and gain strength and courage from his example. They also see death as a new beginning as they look forward to the afterlife.

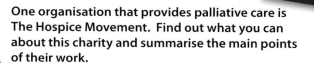

FURTHER THINKING

One organisation that provides palliative care is The Hospice Movement. Find out what you can about this charity and summarise the main points of their work.

EUTHANASIA IN OTHER COUNTRIES

The Netherlands has the most liberal attitude towards euthanasia. Under Dutch law, doctors can administer a lethal dose of muscle relaxants and sedatives to terminally ill patients at a patient's request. The Netherlands Criminal Code Article 293, paragraph two, stipulates that the doctor:

- must be convinced that the patient has made a voluntary and well-considered request to die.
- must be convinced that the patient is facing interminable and unendurable suffering.
- has informed the patient about his situation and his prospects.
- together with the patient, must be convinced that there is no other reasonable solution.
- has consulted at least one other independent doctor who has seen the patient and given his written assessment of the due care requirements as referred to in the points above.
- has helped the patient to die with due medical care.

A euthanasia device in a museum. The device was invented by Dr Phillip Nitschke and facilitated euthanasia through administering heavy doses of drugs. The laptop screen led the user through a series of steps, asking questions to ensure he or she was fully prepared.

This device was legal in Australia's Northern territory between 1995 and 1997.

The case of Daniel James

Daniel James, a 23 year old rugby player, was paralysed in a training session in 2007. Following the accident he loathed his existence in what he said was a 'prison' of his body. According to his mother: "He couldn't walk, had no hand function, but constant pain in all of his fingers. He was incontinent, suffered uncontrollable spasms in his legs and upper body and needed 24-hour care." In 2008 he went to a euthanasia clinic in Switzerland, accompanied by his parents, for an assisted suicide. Following his death, Daniel's parents said he was "an intelligent young man of sound mind" who was "not prepared to live what he felt was a second-class existence."

Those who oppose euthanasia say that Daniel could have learnt to deal with his new life given proper care and support. They point out that he was a young man with his whole life ahead of him. Prior to this case you may have thought that euthanasia was only a concern for the elderly or terminally ill. However, this was a case of a young man wanting the right to die.

Information taken from 'Why Daniel James chose to die', 19 October 2008, *The Times*, www.timesonline.co.uk, accessed 3 April 2009

RELIGIONS AND EUTHANASIA

World religions regard understanding death and dying as vital to finding meaning in human life. Dying is often regarded as a time of preparing for the afterlife. All world faiths have strong views on euthanasia.

Most religions disapprove of euthanasia. Some of them, for example the Roman Catholic Church, completely forbid it. Most religious believers argue that those who become vulnerable through illness or disability deserve care and protection, and that proper care at the end of life is a much better option than euthanasia.

Religions are opposed to euthanasia for a number of reasons. However, at the heart of their opposition is the belief that human life is sacred because God created it. Human life should be protected and preserved, and allowing euthanasia is regarded as murder.

WHAT THE BIBLE SAYS ABOUT EUTHANASIA

The Bible does not directly condemn euthanasia. However, one of the Ten Commandments (Exodus 20:13) forbids murder and most Christians take this to apply to euthanasia. Some Christians argue that there are two occasions when the act of euthanasia is described in the Bible.

Judges 9:52–55
In this account, Abimelech asks to be put to death simply so that he would not suffer the shame of being killed by a woman. The idea that euthanasia is an acceptable practice is not considered.

2 Samuel 1:1–15
This account records the final moments of King Saul who had acted against God's will, and so had lost the right to lead the people. The Amalekite who killed Saul is later put to death by David for doing so. Some argue that David's taking of the Amalekite's life was evidence that his taking Saul's life had been a wrong thing to do. Others argue that

David did this because the Amalekite had killed a king of Israel, not because he had performed 'euthanasia' on someone.

A key Christian belief is that all life is sacred and a gift from God. Life is for living and should be lived to the full. In Ecclesiastes 3:1–8 it is clear that while life can be full of joy and happy times, there will also be times of sadness and suffering. However Christians believe that even in suffering there can be a purpose.

Look at the references in the table below and explain how a Christian might use them in an argument against euthanasia.

Reference	Relevance to euthanasia debate
Genesis 1:27	
Exodus 20:13	
Matthew 9:18–26	
Matthew 9:35–36	
Matthew 18:12–14	
Luke 12:6–7	
Philippians 1:21	
2 Corinthians 5:8	

WHAT THE CHURCHES SAY ABOUT EUTHANASIA

The Roman Catholic Church clearly condemns euthanasia as morally unacceptable:

"It is necessary to state firmly once more that nothing and no one can in any way permit the killing of an innocent human being, whether a foetus or an embryo, an infant or an adult, an old person, or one suffering from an incurable disease, or a person who is dying. Furthermore, no one is permitted to ask for this act of killing, either for himself or herself or for another person entrusted to his or her care, nor can he or she consent to it, either explicitly or implicitly. Nor can any authority legitimately recommend or permit such an action. For it is a question of the violation of the divine law, an offence against the dignity of the human person, a crime against life, and an attack on humanity…The pleas of gravely ill people who sometimes ask for death are not to be understood as implying a true desire for euthanasia; in fact, it is almost always a case of an anguished plea for help and love. What a sick person needs, besides medical care, is love, the human and supernatural warmth with which the sick person can and ought to be surrounded by all those close to him or her, parents and children, doctors and nurses."

Declaration on Euthanasia, Sacred Congregation for the Doctrine of the Faith, 1980

The Presbyterian Church also focuses on the importance of care for the dying:

"Compassion for our fellow human beings means we have the duty to help them die in as comfortable and peaceful ways as we can. We also believe that death is not disaster for those who have committed their lives to Christ. Dying in faith means going to be with him and it is right that we should welcome the release of death for those whose quality of life has been reduced to a daily grind of suffering or infirmity…We believe Christians should urge government and society to adopt the other choices that are available for the alleviation of pain and suffering. Necessary resources should be given to support already successful research into pain relief. Facilities like the Hospice Movement should be encouraged. Above all, the Christian community should take the lead in showing the prayerful, dignified, respectful care which assures people that they are valued and loved, even in the midst of pain and helplessness."

Social Issues and Resources Committee

The Church of Ireland

"…I am not arguing in favour of prolonged suffering…one of the most terrible things that can happen to us, as human beings, is to watch someone we love go through suffering. It is

▶

agony. We want to soothe and cherish them, take away the pain. Our helplessness, if we cannot do so, is appalling; and if the one suffering is our own child, then anguish is piled on anguish. It is awful – no other word will do. It is because many of us have suffered in this way that we can see, at first glance, the reasons why, if someone is suffering terribly with a terminal illness, we might consider euthanasia to be a desirable option…What is needed is not what some are calling, in a horrible travesty of language, the 'therapeutic option' of euthanasia or assisted suicide, but far greater resource – for greater training in palliative care, a care which embraces body, mind and soul."

The Bishop of St Albans, Christopher Herbert, commenting in opposition to the Assisted Dying Bill, 2005

FOR YOUR FOLDER

Summarise the views on euthanasia of some of the main Christian denominations:

Church views on euthanasia		
Roman Catholic	Presbyterian	Church of Ireland

FOR YOUR FOLDER

1. What is euthanasia?

SP09 2. Explain, giving examples, the difference between 'voluntary' and 'involuntary' euthanasia.

3. Explain some of the arguments a Christian might give against voluntary euthanasia.

SP09 4. How might having a strong Christian faith help a person to cope with serious illness?

5. Do you think that quality of life is more important than the number of years you live?

SP09 6. "People should have the right to choose euthanasia if this is what they want." Do you agree or disagree?

7. Some people think that euthanasia is a greater evil than abortion. How might a Christian respond to such a statement?

● CAPITAL PUNISHMENT

Capital punishment or the 'death penalty' is the practice of executing someone as a punishment for a very serious crime, such as murder. It usually follows a legal trial carried out by the state.

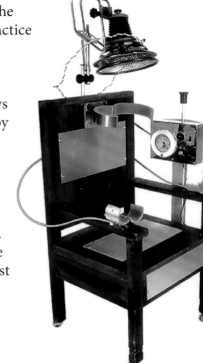

Many people are outraged that the death penalty still exists in some countries. A number of events have taken place which suggest that there is growing support for abolishing capital punishment:

2001 The First World Congress Against the Death Penalty was held in Strasbourg

2002 The World Coalition Against the Death Penalty created in Rome

2003 The First World Day Against the Death Penalty (10 October every year since)

CAPITAL PUNISHMENT AND THE LAW

As a method of punishment, capital punishment is legal in many countries, although many never actually use it. It is used in countries such as China, Pakistan, Iraq, Iran, Sudan and the USA. Look up some states in Amnesty International's website (www.amnesty.org) to see the number of people executed in each of these countries per year.

The following table outlines the arguments for and against capital punishment. Some of the arguments also apply to punishment in general.

ARGUMENTS FOR CAPITAL PUNISHMENT	ARGUMENTS AGAINST CAPITAL PUNISHMENT
Deterrence The argument is that capital punishment is a deterrent to other criminals. It will stop them from committing serious crimes.	1. The death penalty does not deter people from committing serious crimes. The thing that deters is the likelihood of being caught and punished. Statistics show that the death penalty leads to an increase in murder rate. In the USA, more murders take place in states where capital punishment is allowed. 2. Capital punishment also 'lowers the tone' of society. Many people feel that the death penalty is an inappropriate way for a modern civilised society to respond to even the most dreadful crimes.
Retribution It is the ultimate payback for a criminal who has committed an evil act.	1. Many people believe that retribution is wrong. It is revenge, not justice. Capital punishment is a cruel and inhumane way of punishing a criminal. The methods of capital punishment cause unnecessary suffering to a human being, for example, execution by lethal gas, electrocution or strangulation. 2. Many countries that use capital punishment use the lethal injection, believing it to be less cruel for the criminal. But this is unfair on the doctor who has to administer it. It goes against the morals of many in the medical profession. 3. Other people argue that the death penalty is not the ultimate payback. It does not cause enough suffering for a criminal who deserves it. They argue that life imprisonment without the chance of parole would cause much more suffering. 4. What about martyrdom? For example, it can be argued that capital punishment makes convicted terrorists into martyrs. Again, it would be a worse punishment to keep them alive to face a life in prison.
Protection Capital punishment protects society from the criminal by getting rid of an evil person. A person, by their actions, can forfeit human rights and their right to life.	1. Some people argue that human life is so valuable that even the worst criminals should not be deprived of their lives. They argue that everyone has a right to life, even those who commit murder; sentencing a person to death and executing them violates that right. 2. There is also the issue of getting it wrong. Innocent people have been killed, because of mistakes. In the USA, 116 people sentenced to death have been found innocent since 1973 and released from death row. 3. What about people who kill because they are insane? Such people are not responsible for their actions. They should be helped, not convicted, and certainly not executed.
God authorises the death penalty The Bible speaks in favour of the death penalty for murder. A state can act, not on its own authority, but as the agent of God, who has power over life and death.	1. It can also be argued that as God creates life then it should only be God who destroys life. God commanded "*Do not commit murder*" (Exodus 20:13), and that this is a clear instruction with no exceptions. 2. The Bible also prescribes the death penalty for 35 other crimes that society no longer accepts as just. To be consistent, society should remove the death penalty for murder. 3. Christianity in the New Testament is based on forgiveness and compassion. Capital punishment cannot go hand-in-hand with a teaching that emphasises forgiveness and compassion.
Capital punishment is the **cheapest** and most **cost-effective** way of dealing with a serious criminal.	Capital punishment is not cheap. In New York, for example, when the death penalty was reinstated between 1995 and 2004, costs for each person condemned to death were approximately $23 million.

WHAT THE BIBLE SAYS ABOUT CAPITAL PUNISHMENT

Old Testament teaching suggests that God created the death penalty. It lists 36 capital offences, for example, idolatry, magic and blasphemy. Murder is the ultimate capital offence:

> *"Human beings were made like God, so whoever murders one of them will be killed by someone else."*
>
> Genesis 9:6

Capital punishment supports the commandment *"Do not commit murder"* (Exodus 20:13) by affirming the seriousness of the crime of murder.

The Old Testament also seems to permit revenge:

> *"But if the woman herself is injured, the punishment shall be life for life, eye for eye, tooth for tooth, hand for hand, foot for foot".*
>
> Exodus 21:23–24

In the **New Testament** Jesus changed the teaching from the Old Testament that was familiar to his listeners. He taught that Christians should not look for revenge in this way:

> *"You have heard that it was said, 'An eye for an eye, and a tooth for a tooth.' But now I tell you: do not take revenge on someone who wrongs you. If anyone slaps you on the right cheek, let him slap your left cheek too."*
>
> Matthew 5:38–39

In John 8:1–11 we read the story of the woman caught in adultery. The Jewish teachers of the law brought her to Jesus and asked him what he thought should be done to her. The law said that she should be stoned to death. Jesus replied that any of them who had never sinned should throw the first stone. One by one they left until the woman was left with Jesus. He asked, *"'Where are they? Is there no one left*

to condemn you?' 'No one, sir,' she answered. 'Well, then,' Jesus said, 'I do not condemn you either. Go, but do not sin again.'" This passage highlights the need for forgiveness.

IN A GROUP

Do you think Jesus would have said the same if the woman had committed murder, rather than adultery?

It is clear that Jesus himself does not agree with violence. However, at no point does he deny the right of the State to use capital punishment. When Pilate has to decide whether or not to crucify Jesus, Jesus tells him that the power to make this decision has been given to him by God:

> *"You have authority over me only because it was given to you by God."*
>
> John 19:11

The ideal of not taking revenge continues with the writing of Paul in the New Testament:

> *"Ask God to bless those who persecute you—yes, ask him to bless, not to curse…Never take revenge…Do not let evil defeat you; instead, conquer evil with good."*
>
> Romans 12:14–21

Paul advises that judgment should be left to God because:

> *"You will reap exactly what you plant."*
>
> Galatians 6:7

While the tone of the whole of the New Testament is one of forgiveness, Paul in his letters to the Romans seems to refer to the state's right to administer the death penalty:

> *"Everyone must obey state authorities, because no authority exists without God's permission, and the*

existing authorities have been put there by God. Whoever opposes the existing authority opposes what God has ordered; and anyone who does so will bring judgment on himself…They are God's servants and carry out God's punishment on those who do evil."

Romans 13:1–2, 4

WHAT THE CHURCHES SAY ABOUT CAPITAL PUNISHMENT

In the past, the Christian Church accepted capital punishment as a necessary part of the workings of society.

However, there are different views among Christians today regarding the death penalty. They argue both for and against the death penalty using secular arguments, but they often base their case on their religious beliefs.

The Catholic Church

From 1929 to 1969 the law of Vatican City included the death penalty for anyone who tried to assassinate the Pope. In the first half of the twentieth century most Catholic theologians were in favour of capital punishment for serious offenders.

However, as time went on, opinions began to change. The National Conference of Catholic Bishops published a statement in 1980 on capital punishment. It was almost completely negative. In 1997 the Vatican announced changes to the Catechism, which included the following statement about capital punishment:

"Assuming that the guilty party's identity and responsibility have been fully determined, the traditional teaching of the Church does not exclude recourse to the death penalty, if this is the only possible way of effectively defending human lives against the unjust aggressor. If,

however, non-lethal means are sufficient to defend and protect people's safety from the aggressor, authority will limit itself to such means, as these are more in keeping with the concrete conditions of the common good and more in conformity with the dignity of the human person. Today, in fact, as a consequence of the possibilities which the state has for effectively preventing crime, by rendering one who has committed an offence incapable of doing harm – without definitively taking away from him the possibility of redeeming himself – the cases in which the execution of the offender is an absolute necessity are rare, if not practically non-existent."

FOR YOUR FOLDER

1. Explain the different arguments that a Christian might hold both for and against capital punishment. Present your answer in a table.

2. How might some Christians be confused about what they should believe about capital punishment?

3. Do you agree that capital punishment cannot go hand-in-hand with Christian teaching that emphasises forgiveness and compassion?

4. "Bring back the death penalty for all murderers!" Do you think that Christians should support this statement?

FURTHER THINKING

Find out what one of the following Christian denominations believes about capital punishment:

- The Presbyterian Church in Ireland
- The Church of Ireland
- The Methodist Church in Ireland
- The Baptist Church

IN A GROUP

Read the newspaper article opposite, and the opinions that follow. Prepare for a debate:

"This house believes that President Bush was right when he hailed the sentencing of Saddam Hussein to death as a measure of justice for his victims."

President Bush has hailed the sentencing of Saddam Hussein to death as a measure of justice for his victims. He said the verdict was a milestone in the Iraqi people's efforts to replace the rule of a tyrant with the rule of law.

Bush gives his verdict: "It's a major achievement for Iraq's young democracy and its constitutional government. During Saddam Hussein's trial, the court received evidence from 130 witnesses. The man who once struck fear in the hearts of Iraqis had to listen to free Iraqis recount the acts of torture and murder that he ordered against their families and against them. Today, the victims of this regime have received a measure of the justice which many thought would never come."

'Bush on Saddam: a measure of justice', Sky News, 6 November 2006, http://news.sky.com/skynews, accessed 4 April 2009

Around the world there was a varied reaction to Saddam Hussein's guilty verdict and death penalty:

Finland	Acting at the time as current president of the EU.	"The EU opposes capital punishment in all cases and under all circumstances, and it should not be carried out in this case either."
Iran	Mohammad Alihosseini, Iranian Foreign Ministry Spokesman.	"The Islamic Republic of Iran, remembering the inhuman crimes of Saddam and his allies against the Iraqi, Iranian and Kuwaiti nations, and the necessity of preserving the rights of these nations, welcomes the verdict."
Italy	Hands Off Cain, an Italian organisation working to rid the world of capital punishment.	"This is not the way to present the new Iraq to the world, which is different from Saddam, who was behind hundreds of thousands of deaths as well as death penalty sentences."
Kuwait	Abdul-Ridha Aseeri, who heads the political science department at Kuwait University.	"This is justice from heaven. He should have been hanged a long time ago. This is the smallest punishment for someone who executed tens of thousands of people".
Roman Catholic Church	Cardinal Renato Martino, Pope Benedict XVI's top cardinal for justice issues.	"For me, to punish a crime with another crime, which killing for revenge is, means that we are still at the state of 'eye for an eye, tooth for a tooth.' Capital punishment is not a natural death. God gave us life and only God can take it away."
Russia	Kremlin official, Konstantin Kosachyov.	"A death sentence will apparently split Iraqi society even further. On the other hand, it seems to me that the death sentence against Saddam Hussein will probably not be carried out. It will be stopped one way or another, either by the president of Iraq or by other means. It is most of all a moral decision – retribution that modern Iraq is taking against Saddam's regime."
Thailand	Vitaya Wisethrat, a respected Muslim cleric.	"The hanging of Saddam Hussein will turn to hell for the Americans."

PUNISHMENT

If someone commits a crime and they are caught then they are punished. Punishment is there for a reason. Some of the aims of punishment include:

Protection

Society must be protected from dangerous criminals. They lose their freedom so others do not have to worry about being in danger from them.

Deterrent

A sentence may be a deterrent to a criminal repeating the same offence. Others may also be deterred from committing crime when they see what happens to those who offend.

Reform (or rehabilitation)

It aims to reform the criminal so they learn to be a law-abiding member of society. Many Christians believe this is important because Jesus offered forgiveness and hope to those who had offended in his day.

Vindication

People want to see that laws are upheld. Those who break them should be punished to show that society is determined to uphold justice.

Revenge (or retribution)

Society and the victims of a crime deserve to take revenge on the criminal. In the Old Testament Moses laid down the principle of *"eye for eye, tooth for tooth"* (Exodus 21:24). Some Christians support this today. Others disagree and point out that Jesus taught forgiveness.

Repayment (or reparation)

The criminal should make good the damage and hurt they have caused. They might do community service where they carry out useful tasks for society, repay money they have stolen or even apologise to their victim.

If a person is caught they are arrested, go to court and are given a type of punishment that the court decides 'fits the crime'. Christians do not believe punishment is wrong, but many believe punishment should be humane. Prisons, for example, should have decent facilities and should aim to reform the criminal.

Some types of punishment include:

- **A Fine.**

- **Community service** – a certain number of hours in supervised community work.

- **Suspended sentence** – the offender's prison sentence is not carried out so long as they do not offend for the period of the sentence.

- **Probation** – being supervised by a probation officer at regular intervals.

- **Cautioning** – the offender admits the crime and this is recorded. No further action is taken unless the person offends again.

- **Tagging** to check that the offender stays at home, for example, at night. This is called a curfew.

- **Antisocial Behaviour Order (ASBO)** – the offender is warned to keep away from certain areas, activities or people. If he or she fails to do so, the courts will impose a penalty such as a fine or prison.

- **Imprisonment.**

CRIME AND FORGIVENESS

Everyone has a duty to obey the law of the land. If someone breaks the law then they have committed a crime. Christian teaching about repentance and forgiveness is important when it comes to issues of crime and punishment. While it is necessary to punish people for wrongdoing most Christians would agree that there comes a time for forgiveness. Forgiveness is a conscious decision not to feel resentment. It means not ignoring, excluding or acting coldly towards the offender.

Forgiveness is easier if the offender is really sorry

for what they have done and determined not to re-offend. However, if a criminal is not sorry, then forgiveness is a difficult step to take.

Some people find it easy to forgive. They forgive and give the offender another chance. They know that they have forgiven the person because they feel sorrow over the incident, rather than anger. They might even try to understand why the person committed the offence in the first place.

Some crimes are easier to forgive than others. There are two main types of crime:

1. Crimes against the person include murder, assault and sexual offences.
2. Crimes against property include burglary, shoplifting and vandalism.

IN A GROUP

1. Draw two columns representing 'crimes against the person' and 'crimes against property'. List at least five crimes in each column. Do any belong in both?
2. Draw a mind map of methods of punishment. Include a fact about each.
3. If you were to decide, which punishment would you give to each crime?
4. Think about forgiveness. Which crime would be the easiest to forgive and which crime would be the hardest? Rank order the crimes from 1–10 (1 is the easiest to forgive and 10 the hardest).

WHAT THE BIBLE SAYS ABOUT REPENTENCE AND FORGIVENESS

Christians believe it is important to follow Jesus' example of forgiveness. Once a punishment has been carried out, forgiveness and the opportunity to change should be given to the criminal. Jesus gave practical guidelines and clear examples of how he expected his followers to act in a forgiving way. In the Lord's Prayer Christians regularly pray: "Forgive us our trespasses [sins] as we forgive those who trespass against us." This is a reminder that only those who are prepared to forgive can ask for forgiveness for themselves.

The Parable of the Unforgiving Servant (Matthew 18:21–35)

The Parable of the Unforgiving Servant teaches that God will forgive us if we forgive others. A servant owed a king millions of pounds which he could never repay even if he was sold as a slave, along with his wife and family. He would never pay off such a colossal debt. The servant went to the king and promised an impossible task: to repay the king everything. The king, knowing that this was impossible, felt sorry for him and cancelled the debt. The size of the debt shows the extent of the forgiveness.

However, the forgiven servant quickly forgot what the king had done for him and failed to learn from the king's example. After leaving the palace, the servant met a fellow servant who owed him only a few pounds. The first servant refused to be patient with him and threw him into jail. On hearing this, the king immediately withdrew his forgiveness from the unforgiving servant. He reinstated the debt and put him back into jail until he paid it back. This was impossible for the first servant to do.

Jesus stressed that this is exactly what God will do to those who will not forgive from the heart. In other words, if Christians do not practise forgiveness then God will withdraw his mercy.

The Parable of the Lost Son (Luke 15:11–32)

The Parable of the Lost Son teaches Christians that they should forgive someone who repents. It shows that forgiveness should be possible, no matter what crime has been committed.

In the story there was a man who had two sons. The younger took his inheritance, left home and wasted the money in wild living. When he lost everything and was living in desperate poverty he decided to return home and ask his father for forgiveness. When his father saw him coming towards the house he ran out to meet him and organised a celebration feast because his son had come home. The elder son was very angry and jealous. But his father told him to celebrate and be happy for it was as if his brother was dead and now was alive again.

Forgiveness in action

There is a long history of conflict in Northern Ireland between Catholic and Protestant groups. You may have heard of the term 'the Troubles', which used to describe the years of conflict between approximately 1969 and 1998, the year the Good Friday Agreement was signed. During these years over three and a half thousand people were killed.

Gordon Wilson is an example of a Christian who forgave those who had committed a crime against him. In 1987 the IRA bombed a Remembrance Day ceremony in Enniskillen killing 11 people. His daughter was among the dead. Loyalist paramilitaries were intent on retaliation but were stopped by the words of Gordon Wilson:
"I have lost my daughter, and we shall miss her. But I bear no ill

Enniskillen War Memorial was badly damaged in the bomb. It has been restored and a dove added for each of the people who died.

will. I bear no grudge," he told the BBC. "Dirty sort of talk is not going to bring her back to life." He said he forgave her killers and added: "I shall pray for those people tonight and every night." A group called Enniskillen Together was set up to further the cause of reconciliation in the area. On Remembrance Day 1997 the leader of Sinn Fein, Gerry Adams, formally apologised for the bombing.

IN A GROUP

1. How hard do you think it was for Gordon Wilson to forgive the bombers? Give reasons for your answer.

2. Do you think you could forgive such an atrocity?

3. How do you think Gordon was helped by his Christian faith?

FOR YOUR FOLDER

1. Describe three purposes or aims of punishment.

2. How are people punished for the crimes they commit?

3. Explain what Jesus taught in his parables about the importance of forgiveness.

4. Do you think that a Christian should always forgive? Give reasons for your answer.

RESTORATIVE JUSTICE

Restorative Justice is a problem-solving approach to crime which involves:

1. the offender
2. the victim
3. the community

It works to resolve conflict and repair harm by:

- encouraging those who have caused harm to look at the damage they have done.
- giving them an opportunity to make reparation (make things right).
- offering those who have suffered harm the opportunity to have their harm or loss acknowledged and amends made.

The Restorative Justice Consortium (RJC) was formed in 1997 as the national voice for restorative justice in England and Wales. It brings together a wide range of organisations and individuals from across the world with an interest in restorative justice. The RJC aims to promote the use of restorative justice within the criminal justice system, the workplace and schools, to handle situations where conflict occurs. It also develops and promotes agreed principles and standards to guide restorative procedures.

RESTORATION

Those who support restorative justice argue that after a crime has been committed people cannot really move on with their lives without becoming involved with restoration. The word 'restore' can also mean 'repair'. It means fixing things or returning them to their natural state. In this context restoration is concerned with building a better society and affects three groups:

- The victim – restoration of the victim to a normal life.
- The offender – restoration of the offender to a law-abiding life.
- The community – restoration of the damage caused by crime to the community.

The idea is that the needs of victims, offenders and the community are not independent. All three must work together. You might think that this is impossible but restorative justice has been found to work among some non-Western cultures, for example, the native populations of North America (Native American sentencing circles) and New Zealand (Maori justice).

THE LIMITATIONS OF RESTORATIVE JUSTICE

1. One of the limitations of restorative justice is that it relies on voluntary cooperation. If one party does not want to take part then the range of options is reduced. If neither party is willing, there is no option but to let formal justice (the courts) take its usual course. Can you think of some crimes were restorative justice would be particularly difficult?

2. If restorative justice involves the community, then there obviously needs to be a community. However, social injustice and inequality are common in many communities. This limits how communities can be supportive and caring. For example, if there is a big gap between the rich and the poor in a community (social divisions) then there is not likely to be much voluntary participation, as the people are unlikely to want to work together.

HOW RESTORATIVE JUSTICE WORKS IN PRACTICE

The victim and the offender

Meetings are organised to give offenders a chance to take steps to make voluntary reparation (compensation) to their victims. This means much more than paying money to victims, although that may be part of it. It involves:

- an apology and an explanation of how the crime came about. The offender has to listen to the victim's own story and respond to it. Supporters of restorative justice say that this can help victims get over the crime and that it has an impact on the offenders, who have to face up to the reality of what they have done. It helps offenders to restore their own reputations to some extent, and makes them better prepared for joining society by having dealt with their guilt.

- a practical gesture such as financial payments, work for the victim, work for a community cause selected by the victim or an agreement to attend a counselling course.

Meetings deal with victims' emotional, as much as material, needs. Some victims even find it helpful to offer forgiveness in return for the offender's remorse. Any unresolved difficulties between them can also be settled, such as how to behave should they meet one another in the street, any remaining bad feelings or fears, or continuing relationship problems (if, as often happens, they already knew each other).

After a successful meeting both parties can draw a line under the experience. In many cases the victim also experiences satisfaction from influencing the offender away from crime – transforming a negative experience into something positive.

The meetings are carefully carried out by a skilled, specially trained mediator, whose task is to ensure a safe and comfortable environment and to set ground-rules for a positive meeting.

The victim and the community

Community support for victims usually happens through the victims' own personal friends or relatives. Some people don't have this support. The voluntary organisation **Victim Support** exists to fill this gap by offering practical help and support to victims, using available trained volunteers to visit. Victim Support helps to overcome the distrust and sense of being on your own that afflicts many victims of crime. It helps the victim to get over what has happened to them.

Other community groups, such as Women's Aid or Childline, also help victims of crime. There are also self-help support groups for parents of murdered children, victims of drunk drivers, and so on. These voluntary organisations play an important part in restoring victims and are an essential part of community.

The offender and the community

There are many projects in different communities which try to help offenders. Offenders may need help in trying to find jobs, finding somewhere to live, retraining, education, relationships counselling, drug or alcohol counselling, or activities to encourage getting back into society.
Another group of programmes is carried out in

schools. These are mainly concerned with early offending. There are programmes for bullying, truancy, misbehaviour and school exclusions. The programmes are concerned with improving how the schools themselves can deal with their internal problems. They help schools to set up 'dispute resolution' training for pupils, which helps them to avoid trouble arising from arguments, or even to provide their own counselling and mediation services for fellow pupils.

DOES RESTORATIVE JUSTICE WORK?

Research in the UK and elsewhere, has confirmed that about 75% of victims are satisfied with the results of mediation (for example Umbreit & Coates, 1992; Umbreit 1994; Umbreit et al, 1997). Many victims felt less angry and fearful, felt personally vindicated, experienced a degree of emotional healing, and were happy to witness that the offender had not been let off too lightly. Mediation has been shown to have a considerable impact on offenders as well, and in many cases it is thought to have deterred offenders from re-offending.

For Further information: 'Restorative justice: an overview', TF Marshall, A report by the Home Office, Research Development and Statistics Directorate, 1999

FOR YOUR FOLDER

1. What is restorative justice?

2. Explain one of the aims of restorative justice.

3. Why might a Christian be keen to support the idea of restorative justice?

4. Describe some of the limitations of restorative justice.

5. Do you think that restorative justice puts an extra burden on the victim of a crime?

6. Do you think that Christians should be more concerned with the victims of crime rather than with the criminals?

7. "The only decent way to treat a criminal is to lock them up and throw away the key." Do you agree or disagree?

Chapter 3

CARE FOR THE ENVIRONMENT

Christians believe that God created the Earth. The first statement of the Apostles' Creed, which is recited in some Sunday worship services, reads: "I believe in God the Father Almighty, maker of heaven and Earth". God also created human beings (Adam and Eve). He put them in charge of the Garden of Eden and because they lived on the Earth they had responsibility to care for the environment:

"Then God said, 'And now we will make human beings; they will be like us and resemble us. They will have power over the fish, the birds, and all animals, domestic and wild, large and small… Have many children, so that your descendants will live all over the Earth and bring it under their control. I am putting you in charge of the fish, the birds, and all the wild animals.'"

Genesis 1:26&28

"You appointed them rulers over everything you made; you placed them over all creation".

Psalm 8:6

Christians argue that although people live on the Earth, they do not own it. It still belongs to God; it is 'on loan':

"The world and all that is in it belong to the Lord; the Earth and all who live on it are his."

Psalm 24:1

Therefore there is an onus on people to take care of the Earth. In the Old Testament the Jews had responsibility to take care of the land. God gave instructions to them about rest for the environment, especially for the land for growing crops on. They were told to let the land rest once every fifty years so that it would produce more in the future (Leviticus 25:8–11). In times of warfare, instructions were given to conserve fruit trees and not to destroy them when they were attacking a city (Deuteronomy 20:19).

The New Testament also highlights God's concern for earthly life. For example, in Luke's Gospel Jesus talks about the value of plants:

"Look how the wild flowers grow: they don't work or make clothes for themselves. But I tell you that not even King Solomon with all his wealth had clothes as beautiful as one of these flowers. It is God who clothes the wild grass—grass that is here today and gone tomorrow, burned up in the oven. Won't he be all the more sure to clothe you? What little faith you have!"

Luke 12:27–28

Christians today often look to the Bible in praise of creation at harvest time. In some Christian denominations, for example the Presbyterian Church, a Harvest Thanksgiving Service is held every autumn to thank God for the wonder of his creation and provision of their needs.

● STEWARDSHIP

Christians believe that the sin of selfishness has caused neglect and abuse of the environment. The desire to own material things has led people to exploit the Earth rather than take care of it. The idea of accepting responsibility for the Earth and caring for it is known as stewardship. This involves caring for the Earth in the present day, and considering issues for future generations.

FURTHER THINKING

Collect some newspapers over the next few weeks and cut out any stories that talk about the abuse or protection of the environment. Illustrate your findings in a poster.

WHAT THE CHURCHES SAY ABOUT CARING FOR THE ENVIRONMENT

The Methodist Church

"The climate is changing, posing a threat to people everywhere. Already drought and extreme weather are impacting the world's poorest people. The Methodist Church in Ireland recognises the seriousness of the ecological crisis affecting the earth but to stop climate change we need to act now...Concern for the environment is integral to our understanding of faith and arising directly from our theology. It's no longer an optional activity for a busy church...There's no excuse for ignorance...Think about your life and your beliefs. How do you look after creation and how do you love your neighbour? Is your way of life harming others and contributing to the problem?"

www.irishmethodist.org/issues/climate_change.php

The Roman Catholic Church

- The Earth and all life on it is a gift from God given us to share and develop, not to dominate and exploit.
- Our actions have consequences for the rights of others and for the resources of the Earth.
- The goods of the Earth and the beauties of nature are to be enjoyed and celebrated as well as consumed.
- We have the responsibility to create a balanced policy between consumption and conservation.
- We must consider the welfare of future generations in our planning for and utilisation of the Earth's resources.

Pope John Paul 11 in *Sollicitudo Rei Socialis*, 1988

The Church of Ireland

"In the twentieth century, the human impact on the Earth increased enormously. In the last thirty years alone, human activity has destroyed many of the planet's natural resources. Climate change, flooding, habitat destruction, desertification, pollution, urban expansion, and famine have all played their part. A third of all fish species and a quarter of all mammal species are in danger of extinction. One billion people now suffer from a shortage of fresh water...People must be willing to face change and participate actively in the decisions before us all...Greed and over-consumption...must be transformed into generosity and compassion... Both individuals and decision-making bodies of the Church at all levels need to be actively involved in addressing these problems...we ask you...to undertake the following:

- To bring prayers and actions concerning ecology, environmental justice, human rights, and sustainable development to the forefront of public worship.
- To support the struggle of indigenous peoples to maintain their cultural heritage, natural heritage, and human rights.
- To encourage all members of our congregations to understand that God calls us to care for the creation by making our communities and environments better places for the next generation than they were in our lifetime.

- To actively support initiatives that are concerned with the planetary crisis.
- To help publicise information and events among friends, neighbours etc.
- To support opportunities for younger people to experience first-hand how people are affected by the planetary crisis and how they can work to change the world in which they live.
- To promote training and educational programs in all aspects of the planetary crisis.
- To commit ourselves both to energy conservation and the use of sustainable energy sources.
- To demonstrate simplicity of lifestyle in our patterns of consumption to counteract greed and over-consumption."

Declaration to the Anglican Communion

Presbyterian Church

"More and more we are beginning to realise that Environmental problems are the cost of increasing industrialisation, urbanisation, scientific and technological advances. Yet if we are not careful we can be progressing backwards. Increased wealth invariably produces increased waste, more prosperity results in more pollution. God's creation and millions of God's children pay a high price for our so called 'standard of living'…Yet many of our Church members do not feel any biblical imperative to care for God's creation and give little thought to the 'not-so-goodly' heritage which we may be passing on to our children. The Environmental Panel believes that those who are friends of God should also be friends of His creation."

Report of the Panel on the Environment to the 1996 General Assembly

Baptist Church

"We are stewards of creation, responsible for all that God has made, and so a concern for the environment and a just sharing of the world's resources are fundamental gospel commitments… we challenge and encourage our Baptist people to care for the Earth by following sustainable practice and by taking into account global and local environmental considerations for present and future generations:

- in the conservation and use of resources in the church and at home.
- in living in a more sustainable lifestyle.
- in active involvement in community initiatives aimed at sustaining and renewing the environment.
- in concerns for action on global environmental issues."

A Vision for the Environment,
Baptist Union of Great Britain

IN A GROUP

Summarise the issues raised by the different churches. Include how the various churches highlight problems facing the environment and strategies for change. Present your findings in a table.

● CONSERVATION ISSUES

Years ago people thought they had an unending amount of resources to keep the planet going. However, in recent years it has become clear that unless people change their ways the Earth will be under threat. Change is something that is not easy for everyone.

It is estimated one in six people suffer from hunger and malnutrition and that by 2025, two-thirds of the world's people are likely to be living in areas with severe water shortages. The existence of extreme poverty in parts of the world will leave many people no choice but to exploit the environment. It is impossible to expect poor people to respect the environment when they need to use it to survive.

Non-renewable resources such as coal or oil will not be around forever. People depend on oil for 90% of transport, but oil industry experts estimate that current reserves will last only for about 40 years. Experts point out that gas, a suitable replacement for oil, will not last forever either. And while there is still plenty of coal around, it is hard to use without causing high pollution.

All the Christian churches agree that it is time for their members to take responsibility for the environment. Every effort must be made to protect or conserve the environment. Most of the steps that can be taken to conserve energy are the responsibility of the governments around the world. However, there are small changes that people can make in everyday living.

IN A GROUP

Look at the main issues listed in the table below. In groups read about each issue and make a list of practical ways that people can take to conserve energy or protect the environment.

PLANET UNDER THREAT	
Air pollution	Factories release millions of tonnes of chemicals into the air which can harm the environment. Air pollution has been linked to cancer and heart attacks. The World Health Organization (WHO) says three million people are killed worldwide by outdoor air pollution every year and 1.6 million indoors through using solid fuels.
Water pollution	People need fresh water for washing and to drink. Increasing pollution affects the amount of useable water. Rubbish that is buried underground produces poisonous liquids that can enter underground water supplies, causing pollution to people's drinking water. Diseases carried in water are responsible for 80% of illnesses and deaths in developing countries.
Soil pollution	Contaminated land is a problem in industrialised countries, where former factories and power stations can leave waste like heavy metals in the soil. It can also occur in developing countries, sometimes used for dumping pesticides.
Global warming/climate change	The amount of carbon dioxide in the air has increased over the last century because more people than ever are driving cars. The use of electricity, oil and natural gas has also increased. High levels of carbon dioxide turn the atmosphere into a heat trap and so the Earth is becoming warmer. Global weather is changing with extremes of hot and cold, tornadoes, drought, flooding and raging forest fires are often the result.
The ozone layer	A layer of ozone in the atmosphere protects people from the harmful rays of the Sun. Certain gases (CFCs) damage the ozone layer. There is an international ban on the use of CFCs; however, some countries still use them because they are cheap.
Acid rain	Harmful gases such as sulphur dioxide are produced by, for example, cars. Once in the atmosphere these gases combine with water to form 'acid' rain, which kills trees, plants and fish.
E-waste	Old computers, mobile phones and other electronic gadgets are dumped into landfill sites. Computer and TV screens contain lead which is poisonous.
Non-renewable resources	Fossil fuels such as coal and oil have been used extensively to provide energy in our homes.
Renewable resources	There is a danger that forests will become depleted because people are cutting down too many trees. This is also a threat to wildlife.

IT'S TIME TO WAKE UP TO WASTE!

Every year in Northern Ireland people throw away enough waste to cover the whole country. Most of this ends up in landfills, where it is buried and decomposes slowly releasing gases and liquids. Landfills are costly, unattractive and could have a huge impact on the environment and on people's health. There is also the problem of where to have landfill sites. New European legislation requires governments to find better ways of dealing with waste.

You will be very familiar with the following phrase: "Reduce, Reuse and Recycle!" This phrase is known as the 'Three Rs'.

Old Lucozade bottles used as bookends.

THREE RS	
Reduce	Don't produce waste in the first place! It is easy to think about how and why we produce waste and to avoid it.
Reuse	Don't throw things away! Many of the things we throw away could be reused again and again with just a little thought and imagination.
Recycle	Collect things that can be recycled. Many waste products can be turned back into the raw materials they came from and then be used to make new products.

FURTHER THINKING

Find out more at:
http://www.wakeuptowaste.org/
http://www.doeni.gov.uk/index/protect_the_environment/waste.htm

The problems facing the environment affect everyone. Christians believe they have a special responsibility to protect the environment. It is not just to be left to politicians and those with a special interest. There are many simple things that people can incorporate into their everyday lives to make a difference. Here are some examples:

- Switch it off – a TV left on standby can use 85% of the energy it uses when it is actually on.
- Use energy efficient light bulbs.
- Open the kitchen window instead of using the extractor fan.

In groups make a list of some of the other things that people could do.

FOR YOUR FOLDER

Some people may think that environmental issues are not for them. Teenagers may say: "Leave it to the adults to sort out; I have better things to do." The elderly may say: "Leave it to the young people. I'm too old to be thinking about things like that. And I might not have much time left." You can see how difficult it might be to get people involved.

Pretend that you are the minister or priest of an elderly congregation. Many of your church members do not understand about how the planet is under threat and they have shown a lack of interest when you have raised concerns. How can you convince them that they have a duty to care? You have decided to write a leaflet which you will leave in the pews before worship services. Using the following references explain how everyone, no matter what age they are, has a responsibility to do their bit for the environment:

Colossian 3:23; Matthew 6:2; Matthew 6:4; Genesis 1:28; Psalm 119:11; James 1:5; 1 Thessalonians 5:15; 1 Corinthians 4:2

FURTHER THINKING

- Trocaire, Christian Aid, CAFOD (Catholic Agency for Overseas Development), and Tearfund are charitable organisations that carry out aid and development work motivated by faith in a caring creator – God. Find out about the work of one of these organisations locally, nationally and internationally.

- In 1992 the Earth Summit took place in Rio de Janeiro and was attended by representatives ▶

▶ from nations that are working together for conservation. It was one of the largest gatherings of world leaders ever. They accepted that it was vital to take strong action to conserve energy and resources. Ten years later it was followed by the World Summit on Sustainable Development, which took place in Johannesburg, South Africa in 2002. Find out what happened at the 2002 summit and present your findings in a report.

FOR YOUR FOLDER

1. In the creation story, who did God put in charge of the Garden of Eden?

2. What is meant by 'stewardship'?

3. Name two ways people have mistreated the Earth.

4. Explain how Christians could put what they believe about the environment into practice.

5. How can people give thanks to God for his creation and provision?

6. Do you think church teaching influences Christian attitudes towards the environment?

● ANIMAL RIGHTS

Included in the discussion about caring for the environment is care for animals. Throughout history, people, even Christians, have treated animals in ways that suggest that they do not believe that animals have rights. For example, animals have been hunted, used for circus entertainment, kept in zoos and used for medical research. There are different opinions about whether such treatment of animals is acceptable or not.

ANIMALS FOR FOOD

Most people believe that it is acceptable to use animals for food, as long as the animals are treated humanely in the process. In the UK and Ireland it is acceptable to eat certain animals. Pork, beef, lamb, chicken and fish form part of the diet of most people in our community. Other people are vegetarian. This means that they do not eat meat at all.

FAMOUS VEGETARIAN – SIR PAUL McCARTNEY

The former Beatle and superstar Paul McCartney became a vegetarian after watching lambs play in a field outside his home:
"The surprising thing is that even though many of us, including me, were brought up as traditional meat and fish eaters, it is a simple matter these days, and an exciting one, to consider changing your diet to a healthier one which not only brings benefits to the person who does it, but also to the planet as a whole."

'Turn vegetarian to fight global warming', Sky News, 22 April 2008, http://news.sky.com/skynews, accessed 5 April 2009

Find Out…
What other famous people are vegetarians?

IN A GROUP

Plan a week's evening meals using only vegetarian dishes. Are you a vegetarian? Could you be a vegetarian? What are the advantages and disadvantages of being vegetarian?

ANIMALS FOR RESEARCH

It is widely known and accepted by many that animals are used for experimentation. Animals are used for medical research and to test the safety of other products. Scientists may want to find out if a new medicine works without testing it on a human first. It is argued that because the results will produce great benefits for people, then it is morally acceptable to harm a few animals.

However, many of these experiments cause severe pain to the animals involved and some people say that this is morally wrong and that testing should be banned. But scientists stress that banning animal experiments would mean using people for all tests or else ending testing new drugs altogether. They argue that the good done to human beings ▶

outweighs the harm done to animals, and insist that they try to make sure that such experiments are as humane as possible.

FURTHER THINKING

In 1997 **Dr Jay Vacanti** grew an ear on the back of a mouse. Find out what you can about this experiment. Do you think it was the right thing to do?

ANIMALS AS COMPANIONS

Many breeds of certain animals, for example dogs and cats, have a long history of being human companions. A number of people in your class will have a pet dog or cat or some other animal. Every year people spend a lot of money on their pets, providing them with a loving home. Keeping pets gives many people great happiness, helps them to exercise and provides them with company if they live on their own.

However, some pet owners do not care for their animals and are even cruel to them. In 2007 the Animal Welfare Act came into force. The act toughened penalties for neglect and cruelty, including fines of up to £20,000, a maximum jail term of 51 weeks and a lifetime ban on some owners keeping pets. The Act also places a 'duty of care' on pet owners to provide for their animals' basic needs, such as food and water, veterinary treatment and an appropriate environment in which to live.

IN A GROUP

A pet can be a great friend. List the advantages and disadvantages of owning a pet.

WORKING ANIMALS

Some animals are used for work, for example working dogs on a farm, horses pulling a plough and guide dogs for the blind. Other animals are used for entertainment to bring money in for their owners. Most of you will probably have visited a zoo or been to a circus. Many of the animals there are kept in cages or are trained to perform in front of an audience.

ANIMALS AND HUNTING

Hunting with dogs is a major sport in the UK and Ireland. The animals that are hunted include foxes, deer, mink, rabbits and hares. Although fox hunting is banned in England, Scotland and Wales, a number of people are outraged that hunting is still legal in Northern Ireland. They argue that it is morally wrong to kill for pleasure. Many animals suffer pain and fear during the chase and are often killed painfully. Those animals that manage to escape may be

injured and face a painful and prolonged death.

Hunters disagree arguing that being hunted by other animals is a natural part of the life of wild animals. Some would even say that they are doing the animals a favour because hunting with dogs provides a very quick death and less painful death than being killed in the wild. Traditionally hunting was a form of pest-control. Farmers often welcomed hunters onto their land to protect their livestock by reducing 'pest' numbers. Some farmers still approve of hunting today for this reason.

ILLEGAL DOG-FIGHTING

In 2007 more than 200 dogs, bred for fighting were seized in a crackdown on illegal dog-fighting in Northern Ireland. The dogs, mainly pit bull breeds, were kept in illegal kennels in the region.

Stephen Philpott, a spokesman for the Ulster Society for the Prevention of Cruelty to Animals, said "It's a mind-blowing number of dogs in such a small country...Organised dog fighting is at epidemic proportions in Northern Ireland...the animals live a life of constant misery."

'Animals seized in dog-fight crackdown', 23 August 2007, Sky News, http://news.sky.com/skynews, accessed 3 April 2009

IN A GROUP

Consider the following issues concerning the rights of animals. Draw a table. On the left list those things that you think are acceptable. On the right list the things that you find unacceptable. Discuss your opinions in a group:

- Experiments on animals
- Rearing and killing animals for food
- Rearing and killing animals for fur/leather goods
- Hunting
- Entertainment
- Zoos
- Pet-keeping
- Dog-fighting

Acceptable treatment of animals	Unacceptable treatment of animals	Not sure – give reasons

ANIMAL ACTIVISTS

Most animal rights activists are concerned with preventing cruelty to animals. Some examples of such cruelty include:

- keeping animals in an inappropriate environment – fish in bowls or small tanks, large dogs in small flats or birds in small cages.
- not treating animals well – insufficient exercise, insufficient space, lack of veterinary care, cruelty, neglect and abandonment.
- using animals for painful experiments.

Animal activists live their lives in an animal-friendly way and use acceptable means to promote animal rights. These include not eating animal products; avoiding products tested on animals or made with leather or fur; avoiding zoos and circuses; lobbying the government for pro-animal legislation; and campaigning about animal issues.

ANIMAL EXTREMISTS

Many people confuse animal activists with animal extremists. Animal extremists are campaigners against the use of the cruel treatment of animals and who believe in taking direct action and even use violence. Some of the tactics they use include:

- damaging the premises of organisations that are regarded as anti-animal, such as laboratories or fur farms, or vandalising the homes of those who work there.
- staging protests at laboratories or fur farms.
- releasing animals from captivity.
- sending threatening letters or making harassing telephone calls.
- spreading false rumours.
- physical assaults.

IN A GROUP

"Animal activists are not really committed to the cause of animal rights. Animal extremists show that they are the only ones who really care!" Do you agree or disagree? Give reasons for your answer.

WHAT THE BIBLE SAYS ABOUT THE TREATMENT OF ANIMALS

The Garden of Eden (Genesis 2:4b–20) is an example of God's ideal world, in which human beings lived in peace and harmony with animals. However, other teaching in the Old Testament suggests that animals take second place to human beings:

> *"[God] blessed them, and said, 'Have many children, so that your descendants will live all over the Earth and bring it under their control. I am putting you in charge of the fish, the birds, and all the wild animals.'"*
>
> Genesis 1:28

Some Christians argue that this proves that God has given people the right to treat animals whatever way they want. However, there is other evidence in the Old Testament to suggest that people should not be cruel to animals:

> *"If an Israelite's donkey or cow has fallen down, don't ignore it; help him get the animal to its feet again."*
>
> Deuteronomy 22:4

> *"If you happen to find a bird's nest in a tree or on the ground with the mother bird sitting either on the eggs or with her young, you are not to take the mother bird."*
>
> Deuteronomy 22:6

> *"Do not muzzle an ox when you are using it to thresh grain."*
>
> Deuteronomy 25:4

> *"Good people take care of their animals, but wicked people are cruel to theirs."*
>
> Proverbs 12:10

The prophet Isaiah describes the Kingdom of Heaven as a place where animals and human beings live together in peace:

> *"Wolves and sheep will live together in peace, and leopards will lie down with young goats. Calves and lion cubs will feed together, and little children will take care of them."*
>
> Isaiah 11: 6–7

Jesus told human beings to be kind to the weak and helpless. Some Christians argue that this includes animals that are often weak and helpless. Jesus' teaching in general shows respect for animals:

> *"Aren't five sparrows sold for two pennies? Yet not one sparrow is forgotten by God."*
>
> Luke 12:6

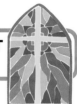

WHAT THE CHURCH SAYS ABOUT THE TREATMENT OF ANIMALS

In the past Christians were guilty of ignoring animal suffering. Many Christian thinkers believed that human beings were greatly superior to animals. For example, Thomas Aquinas taught that a hierarchy exists in the universe. In this hierarchy human beings are above animals and so have the right to use animals in any way they want. Other leading Christians had more respect for animals. At the other extreme is St Francis of Assisi, who gave up his wealth to be a monk. He preached to the birds and became the patron saint of animals. He said that animals deserved protection, respect and even worship.

Christians today believe they are 'stewards' of the environment which includes being kind to animals. They also regard any unnecessary mistreatment of animals as morally wrong and sinful.

The Catholic Church believes that animals are special and should be cared for:

> *"It is necessary and urgent to abandon ill-considered forms of dominating custody of*

Statue of St Francis of Assisi

all creatures. I am happy to encourage and to bless all those who work so that animals may be considered and treated in a Franciscan way, as brothers and sisters…Scientists must abandon laboratories and factories of death."

Pope John Paul II

Christians believe that people should be kind to animals. Church leaders often point to the examples of saints like St Francis of Assisi or St Philip Neri. Find out what you can about these saints.

DO ANIMALS HAVE RIGHTS?	
Animals have rights	Animals do not have rights
Animals should be treated in the way that is best for the animals concerned – which may not be the way that suits human beings. It is wrong for human beings to use animals for food, clothing, experiment or anything else.	Animals were put on Earth to serve human beings. Animals do not have souls. Animals do not behave morally. Animals cannot think morally.

FURTHER THINKING

Write an article on one of the following organisations:

- Catholic Concern for Animals (an international animal welfare society) – www.all-creatures.org/
- Vegetarian Society – http://www.vegsoc.org/
- RSPCA – http://www.rspca.org.uk/
- People for the Ethical Treatment of Animals – http://www.peta.org/
- International Fund for Animal Welfare – http://www.ifaw.org/ifaw/general/default.aspx
- Uncaged – http://www.uncaged.co.uk/
- League Against Cruel Sports – http://www.league.uk.com/

FOR YOUR FOLDER

1. Describe three ways in which animals can be mistreated.

2. How might biblical teaching influence a Christian's attitude to the rights of animals?

3. Explain the difference between an animal activist and an animal extremist.

4. "There is little the Christian Church can do to protect the rights of animals." Do you agree or disagree?

Chapter 4

EQUALITY

The first two Articles of the **United Nations Declaration of Human Rights** (1948) declare:

Article 1
All human beings are born free and equal in dignity and rights. They are endowed with reason and conscience and should act towards one another in a spirit of brotherhood.

Article 2
Everyone is entitled to all the rights and freedoms set forth in this Declaration, without distinction of any kind, such as race, colour, sex, language, religion, political or other opinion, national or social origin, property, birth or other status.

IN A GROUP

Select the key words from these two articles that describe what life should be like for all people everywhere. Copy them down and explain what they mean. Discuss:

Is this what life is like...
*   For you?
*   For your neighbour?
*   For the people of Northern Ireland?
*   For the world at large?

The Declaration of Human Rights describes the ideal way that people should live. However, we live in a world where many people are poor and suffering, while others are very rich and live very comfortable lives. We live in a world that is no stranger to religious, racial and sexual discrimination. Many people are pushed to the edge of society and made to feel as if they have nothing to offer.

SOCIAL JUSTICE

The idea of equality is related to respect for justice. Justice is the right to be treated fairly. Most people care deeply about justice for themselves and others. If we are treated unfairly or we see others being treated badly we may experience a sense of *injustice* and want to do something about it. We are also likely to feel negative emotions such as hate, envy, resentment, anger, vengeance and fear.

Most people want to believe that the world we live in is a place where people get what they deserve or, even, deserve what they get. Unfortunately, this is not the case. Incidents of discrimination, violence and criminal acts are part of everyday life for many. Some of these incidents affect how we live in groups in society. In America there is a history of division between blacks and whites. In Northern Ireland a similar split has existed between Catholics and Protestants. Other examples can be found in South Africa and the Middle East. Each group has a list of historical wrongs and their own demands for justice.

Social justice is an important concept in many aspects of life, including religion, politics, the workplace and society in general. There are a number of ways in which people are not treated fairly and equally in society. You only have to turn on the television or look at a newspaper to realise this. Some examples of social injustice are outlined on the following pages.

TYPES OF SOCIAL INJUSTICE

Social injustice can take many forms. Each type is an example of how people are not treated equally in society.

ECONOMIC INEQUALITY

One of the main forms of social injustice is economic inequality. This refers to the unfair gap between the rich and the poor. In our world some people live in complete luxury while others struggle to survive in dire poverty. People living in developing countries often have a very poor standard of living: they have little chance of getting an education; have no access to modern medical care; and little or no opportunities to use technology. Christians believe that this is wrong. Everyone should have the opportunity to enjoy the wealth that God's world has to offer.

Slums in Mumbai

Poor people are not just those living in poor countries. Many people in the UK and Ireland live in poverty, with barely enough to live on. Care for the poor has always been an important part of Christianity. Many Christians believe it is part of their religious duty to help the poor. They follow the example of Jesus who reached out to the poor in society. There are a number of Christian charities which try to improve the conditions of poor people, for example, Christian Aid, the Salvation Army and CAFOD (Catholic Agency for Overseas Development).

INEQUALITY OF THE DISABLED

Many people in our society are either physically or mentally disabled. Disabled people have a lot to offer society. A number of disabled people live on their own, go out to work and live a reasonably independent life. However, as well as coping with their disability, some face discrimination in society and are not treated as equals. This is a particular problem when it comes to applying for a job or taking part in sports.

GENDER INEQUALITY

Gender inequality refers to the obvious or hidden difference between people based on their gender. Some people believe that women are still not treated equally to men in society. They argue that women are affected by gender inequality in education, the world of work, religion and sport. Such people believe, for example, that men are often given jobs because they are male, even if a better qualified female has also applied for the job. However, other people argue that more recently the situation has reversed. Upon applying for jobs, some men believe they will not be hired for the position because employers are afraid of appearing gender biased against women and that a woman will be hired instead.

In the home women have traditionally carried out the majority of the domestic chores and are responsible for childcare. Women's role within Western society has dramatically changed over the last 100 years, with more women becoming focused on their careers and some even taking over the role as the family bread-winner. It is also more common for men to carry out their share of the household tasks and childcare.

In the Christian Church men have traditionally been the leaders with women taking a lesser role. Women are gradually being selected for higher roles within the church, with some Christian denominations more open to women in leadership roles than others. The Presbyterian Church has been ordaining women into the ministry since 1973 and the Methodist Church in Ireland has had women ministers since 1977. However, it is only in more recent years that the Church of Ireland has allowed women to become priests and in the Catholic Church although women can become nuns or religious sisters, only men can become priests.

IN A GROUP

Discuss the influence of television and advertising in developing gender stereotypes within society.

AGEISM

Ageism is discrimination against people because they are no longer young. Older people are often looked down upon by those younger than them and some even consider them to be of little value to society, with old-fashioned views. Unfortunately these ideas are reinforced by television and advertising. Many older people face discrimination when they try to find work or feel pressurised to retire to make way for younger people. Old people are sometimes made to feel that they are a burden on their families. Christians believe that they should show respect for the elderly and value their experience of life. Many old people are active, valuable to the community and proud of their individuality. More old people could be helped to be like this if opportunities were offered to them that would use their skills and talents, as well as

providing them with a sense of value to the society in which they live. Two organisations committed to improving the quality of life for the elderly are **Age Concern** and **Help the Aged**. Find out what services these charities provide. There is also concern among many in our society that those people who served in the First and Second World Wars (war veterans) should be respected and remembered for the great sacrifice that they made.

RACIAL INEQUALITY

This refers to the unfair treatment of people because they belong to a particular race or because of the colour of their skin. It is a world-wide problem. In America in the 1960s black people were treated as

Coloured drinking fountain, Oklahoma, mid-twentieth century

second class citizens. They were separated from white people in places like schools and restaurants and were victimised by an organisation called the Ku Klux Klan. Find out what you can about this group.

Racial inequality still exists throughout the world today. You will learn more about it in the section that begins on page 60.

RELIGIOUS INEQUALITY

This refers to the unfair treatment of people because they belong to a particular religion. It can affect people from any religion, for example, Christians, Muslims or Jews. In the 1930s Adolf Hitler, the leader of the Nazi party in Germany, tried to exterminate all Jewish people. Over six million Jews died, most of them in the gas chambers of concentration camps. This is known as the Holocaust.

In Northern Ireland religious inequality has been a problem for Catholics and Protestants. In recent years many innocent Muslims face discrimination because of the terror activities of Muslim extremists.

IN A GROUP

Make a poster to illustrate the different types of social injustice in our society. Cut photographs and comments from newspapers and magazines.

WHAT THE BIBLE SAYS ABOUT SOCIAL JUSTICE

The Bible provides insight into how Christians should not tolerate social injustice.

The Old Testament teaches that people are created in God's image (Genesis1:26–27, Psalm 139:3–14) and that all people are created equal. People were not created to be alone, but to live in community with others (Genesis 2:18). People were given a special role in creation – to be stewards of the Earth, to work and to prosper (Genesis1:28–30).

Christians believe that God's creation was spoiled by violence, selfishness, greed and corruption when sin entered the world (Genesis 3–11). The issue of injustice is connected to sin throughout the Old Testament (Isaiah 59:9–16). Many of the prophets spoke out against the social injustice caused by sin and warned the people of coming judgment (Amos 5:11–15, Jeremiah 22:13–17, Isaiah 3:13–15, Habakkuk 2:9–14, Micah 2:1–2).

Amos spoke harshly about people who harm and ill-treat the poor and needy:

"Listen to this, you that trample on the needy and try to destroy the poor of the country. You say to yourselves, 'We can hardly wait for the holy days to be over so that we can sell our grain. When will the Sabbath end, so that we can start selling again? Then we can overcharge, use false measures, and fix the scales to cheat our customers. We can sell worthless wheat at a high price. We'll find someone poor who can't pay his debts,

not even the price of a pair of sandals, and we'll buy him as a slave.' The Lord, the God of Israel, has sworn, 'I will never forget their evil deeds.'"

Amos 8:4–7

The story of Naboth's Vineyard (1 Kings 21) provides teaching on how the poor should be treated. King Ahab is persuaded by his wife Jezebel to arrange for Naboth to be killed. Naboth is much poorer than Ahab but he has some land that the king wants. God sends Elijah to warn Ahab of a terrible judgment. God will not tolerate such social injustice.

Isaiah also speaks out against the oppression of the poor:

"The kind of fasting I want is this: Remove the chains of oppression and the yoke of injustice, and let the oppressed go free. Share your food with the hungry and open your homes to the homeless poor. Give clothes to those who have nothing to wear, and do not refuse to help your own relatives."

Isaiah 58:6–7

There were also special laws to protect widows and orphans (Deuteronomy 24:19); expectations that kings were expected to rule justly (Deuteronomy 17:14–17, Proverbs 31:8–9); and a passion for justice in the Psalms (Psalm 45:6–7).

In the **New Testament** social justice is also an important theme. It is significant that when Jesus was born the angels announced his birth to the poor shepherds, not to the rich people. The shepherds were the first people to visit the baby in Bethlehem. John the Baptist, who prepared the way for Jesus, was concerned with injustice, just like the Old Testament prophets before him (Luke 3:10–14). Jesus, too, challenged the injustice of the powerful Pharisees (Luke 11:42) and brought wholeness and healing to the marginalised. Jesus identified with the poor during his ministry. His teaching on the Kingdom of God revealed that it was a place for the poor and the outcast. When a rich man asked Jesus what he should do to enter the Kingdom, Jesus told him to sell his possessions and give the proceeds to the poor (Mark 10:17–22). Jesus taught his disciples to *"Love your neighbour as you love yourself."* (Mark 12:30–31). The importance of caring for the needy is also in the teachings of Paul (Galatians 2:10), John (1 John 3:16–18) and James (James 1:27).

CHRISTIAN TEACHING ON WEALTH

Jesus stressed that being wealthy is not easy:

> *"It is much harder for a rich person to enter the Kingdom of God than for a camel to go through the eye of a needle."*
>
> Luke 18:25

Christianity does not teach that it is wrong to be rich. However, it does stress that having money is wrong if the desire for money takes over a person's life, or if it is gained dishonestly.

> *"But those who want to get rich fall into temptation and are caught in the trap of many foolish and harmful desires, which pull them down to ruin and destruction. For the love of money is a source of all kinds of evil. Some have been so eager to have it that they have wandered away from the faith and have broken their hearts with many sorrows."*
>
> 1 Timothy 6:9–10

Jesus taught people to look after one another:

> *"I was hungry and you fed me, thirsty and you gave me a drink; I was a stranger and you received me in your homes, naked and you clothed me; I was sick and you took care of me, in prison and you visited me."*
>
> Matthew 25:35–36

The early Church was a radical community that that tried to put Jesus' teachings about justice into practice:

> *"All the believers continued together in close fellowship and shared their belongings with one another. They would sell their property and possessions, and distribute the money among all, according to what each one needed."*
>
> Acts 2:44–45

● THE CHRISTIAN'S RESPONSIBILITY TOWARDS DISADVANTAGED GROUPS

Some Christians believe that there is no divide between the religious and the secular world. Therefore faith and the fight for justice go hand-in-hand. This means that Christians have a responsibility to help disadvantaged groups in our society and beyond.

One of the main ways Christians show their responsibility towards disadvantaged groups is in their attitude towards the poor. Many Christians living in rich nations feel they have a moral responsibility towards those less fortunate. This does not just mean remembering them in prayer, but offering practical help. Many are involved in charities such as Christian Aid, CAFOD (Catholic Agency for Overseas Development), CARITAS (Catholic Agency for International Aid and Development) and Tearfund. These charities try to stop millions of people starving in poorer countries while the rest of the world is well-fed.

People also get involved locally. Soup kitchens are set up in city centres for the homeless. In Belfast an SOS bus helps those who find themselves stranded, in need or distressed late at night. At Christmas, often one of the loneliest times for many people, Christians reach out to the less fortunate by providing companionship, food and toys for families that cannot afford them.

Not everyone can be actively involved in the practical work of helping the needy. There are other ways to help. Some people sponsor a child in a developing country by donating a regular amount of money each month. Others give money to organisations such as the Red Cross. In everyday living Christians can fight against injustice. For example, the Bible teaches that Christians should earn their living in an honest way that does not exploit other people. Christians can also take a stand against the exploitation of women through prostitution and pornography.

LIBERATION THEOLOGY

In South America a movement called Liberation Theology emerged in the 1960s. It was made up of Christians who were convinced that the church should fight against poverty and exploitation, and act to bring about social justice. It was a radical movement with a strong following among Catholic priests in Latin America, Asia and Africa. Many believed the church should become involved with the working class to do so. Some priests, for example, moved from their own houses into poverty stricken areas to share the living conditions.

Liberation theology was based on biblical teaching:

> *"The Spirit of the Lord is upon me, because he has chosen me to bring good news to the poor. He has sent me to proclaim liberty to the captives and recovery of sight to the blind, to set free the oppressed."*
>
> Luke 4:18

Liberation theology also stressed that Christians should take positive action to fight against the misuse of power by governments. Some supporters have been prepared to break the law in order to help ordinary people who are suffering from oppression.

FOR YOUR FOLDER

1. What is social justice?

2. How might a priest or minister convince the congregation that they have a duty to stand up for social justice?

3. Explain what is meant by Liberation Theology.

4. Do you think the church is doing enough to help groups in society that suffer from inequality?

FURTHER THINKING

Choose one of the following groups of people who are disadvantaged or excluded in our society. Find out about a charity or organisation that tries to help them. Present your findings in a PowerPoint presentation.

- The disabled
- The homeless
- Travellers
- The elderly

ISSUES ARISING FROM RACISM AND DISCRIMINATION

Racism means treating people differently because of their race or the colour of their skin. Christianity teaches that everyone is equal in the eyes of God and so it is wrong to make anyone feel inferior or suffer because of differences between them.

If a person is a racist it means they have formed a prejudice against someone because of their race. Prejudice is the act of pre-judging someone, and usually implies judging another person to be of less worth or value, based on little or no actual knowledge of them. If you pre-judge a person because of the colour of their skin, then you are a racist.

Prejudice starts in the mind. You may be prejudiced against a person but keep your thoughts to yourself and do nothing about it. However, some people put their prejudice into action. This is called discrimination. Discrimination is when people are treated badly by others because of prejudice.

Prejudice is an attitude… discrimination is an action

Racism exists all over the world. Your first thought is probably that racism only exists in places like South Africa or America. For example, many of you will be familiar with the work of Martin Luther King. He was a black American Christian who believed that God created everyone, black and white people, to be equal. He worked for equality through non-violent protests, campaigning against the fact that black and white people had separate schools, restaurants and seats on buses. He gave many speeches protesting against injustice. In 1963, in one of his most famous speeches he said:

"I have a dream that my four little children will one day live in a nation where they will not be judged by the color of their skin but by the content of their character."

Forty-five years later his dream started to come true with the election of Barack Obama as the first black president of the United States of America.

RACISM IN NORTHERN IRELAND

You may think that racism is a problem that exists elsewhere but not in your own home town. You would be wrong. In recent years, Northern Ireland has experienced significant economic growth alongside fast changes in the culture and race of the people who live here. A great number of people and their families have moved to Northern Ireland to live, work and learn alongside people who were born here. This is called demographic change.

People who move to Northern Ireland from other countries often bring with them their own culture and religion. They are sometimes referred to as ethnic minorities. A person who belongs to an ethnic minority is someone from a certain race, religion or nationality who lives in a country where the majority of the population belong to a different race, religion, or nationality. For example, white people in China would be considered an ethnic minority just like people of Chinese race would be considered an ethnic minority in Northern Ireland, because the people here are mostly white. A number of ethnic minority communities have been in Northern Ireland for a long time. Many people believe that these minorities have only just arrived in Northern Ireland and do not realise that many ethnic minority members were born here. Some even have Northern Ireland accents!

While the experience of ethnic minorities has been positive, in recent years incidents of racism and discrimination have increased in Northern Ireland, affecting adults, young people and children. It is not just a case of childish name calling. Many people face blatant discrimination, intimidation and even violence. Such people are attacked because of the colour of their skin or their foreign language. Some, for example Muslims, are attacked because of

their religion. Part of the problem behind racism against Muslims is the way they are perceived following the terrorist attacks of 9 September 2001.

Most of these attacks are not reported to the police for fear that it will make things worse. Many people are faced with verbal abuse, stonings, dogs being set loose, face-to-face threats and cars being vandalised. Those attacked say that the vast majority of people in Northern Ireland are kind and tolerant. It is only a small minority who are racist.

Examples of racism in Northern Ireland

1. Frank Kakopa, a structural engineer originally from Zimbabwe, was working in England and brought his wife and children on a mini-break to Northern Ireland in 2005. He had lots of documentary evidence that he was living legally in the UK. However, he was singled out by the Immigration Service and held for two days in Maghaberry Prison. He was strip-searched, isolated from his family and not allowed to make phone calls.

> "I was locked up with convicted criminals, having committed no crime, while my wife and young children were left abandoned at the airport of a strange country worrying about where I was and how I was being treated."

Listeners to Radio Ulster's Sunday Sequence were horrified to hear Mr Kakopa talk about the humiliation he felt: "Being a former prisoner will always stick with me." He was later awarded £7,500 compensation for wrongful imprisonment. Eileen Lavery of the Equality Commission asks a valid question: "Why pick on him? Other than, I think, because he is black."

2. Fransuer comes from Africa and teaches Religious Education in a school in Belfast. He describes how life has been since living in Northern Ireland:

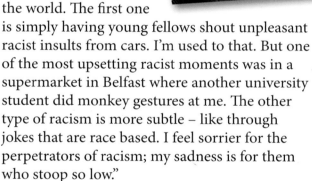

> "Generally this is a great place to live in. However about 5% of people I've come across are racist. There are two main obvious types of discrimination that I have faced in this part of the world. The first one is simply having young fellows shout unpleasant racist insults from cars. I'm used to that. But one of the most upsetting racist moments was in a supermarket in Belfast where another university student did monkey gestures at me. The other type of racism is more subtle – like through jokes that are race based. I feel sorrier for the perpetrators of racism; my sadness is for them who stoop so low."

Fransuer talks of subtle forms of racism. This is echoed in the following statement by the Rev Arlington Trotmann, Secretary of the Churches Together in Britain and Ireland Commission for Racial Justice:

> "We are all aware of the physical and verbal racial attacks. However, more subtle forms of racial discrimination, indifference and overlooking can exist throughout people's lives, in contacts with official bodies, in the schoolroom, job hunting and the workplace, medical and housing services, and socially."

IN A GROUP

Using the examples on page 61, draw a table with two columns. On one side list examples of blatant racist acts; on the other list examples of the more subtle forms of racial discrimination.

The Chinese community in Northern Ireland

The Chinese Community is the largest ethnic minority group in Northern Ireland. The majority of Chinese people live in the Greater Belfast area, although many are scattered throughout the North. They have been in Northern Ireland since the early 1960s.

A high proportion of the Chinese living in Northern Ireland were born outside the country. Most Chinese people come to work, mainly in restaurants, or to study. The Chinese are even more isolated from the rest of the population because of the long unsociable hours associated with restaurants.

Most Chinese people do not go to a church the way Christians do. To them religion is more a personal thing. Some may be influenced by Taoism (ancestor worship) or Buddhism, although very few Chinese living here strictly practice these faiths. However, some of the Chinese people in Northern Ireland are Christians.

Racial harassment is a major problem for the Chinese Community in Northern Ireland, affecting children, adults and the elderly. In a survey of Chinese teenagers born in Northern Ireland from South and East Belfast it was discovered that 100% had experienced some kind of racially motivated attacks, both verbal and physical. Many admitted that they felt treated as unwelcome visitors despite the fact they were born here. Attacks can take the form of physical, mental and verbal abuse, threatening language, stone throwing, spitting and robbery.

Information taken from The Chinese Welfare Association in Belfast, http://www.cwa-ni.org/, accessed 2 April 2009

Filipinos

The Philippines is a country made up of over 7,000 islands, located in the southern hemisphere, south east of China. Many people from other parts of the world, such as the Philippines, are invited to come to the UK and Ireland to work. For example, Ireland has a real shortage of nurses and has invited many well-trained nurses from the Philippines to fill the vacancies. However, some of these Filipinos have not always received a warm welcome in Irish communities and have faced racist attacks.

Polish

Polish people form the largest of the eastern-European immigrant communities in Northern Ireland. Many of them are Catholic, and a Polish Chaplaincy in Ireland was inaugurated in Dublin in 2006. Mass is celebrated in Polish in many towns throughout Northern Ireland.

FURTHER THINKING

In groups choose one of the following organisations representing minority groups. Find out what you can about how this group has faced discrimination in Northern Ireland and what is being done to support the group. You could either write to the contact person or use the internet to gather your information. Report back to the rest of the class.

NI African Cultural Centre, 12 Upper Crescent, Belfast, BT7 1NT Tel: 028 9023 8742	Bangladeshi Welfare Association, Mr Abdul Rob, 24 Greenwell Street, Newtownards, BT23 7LN Tel: 028 9181 0566	Al-Nisa Association NI, Mrs AS Khan, Chairperson, C/O 46 Mount Eden Park, Belfast, BT9 6RB 028 9022 8135
Northern Ireland Muslim Family Association, Dr Mamoun Mobayod, Chairperson, 4 Thornhill Manor, Belfast, BT17 9RB Tel: 07768 028072 http://www.nimfa.org	The Chinese Welfare Association (Northern Ireland), 133–135 University Street, Belfast, BT7 1HP Tel: 028 9028 8277, or email Anna Lo: cwa.anna@cinni.org	The Multicultural Resource Centre, 9 Lower Crescent, Belfast, BT7 1NR Tel: 028 9024 4639 www.mcrc-ni.org
NICEM (Northern Ireland Council for Ethnic Minorities), Ascot House, 24-31 Shaftsbury Square, Belfast, BT2 7BD Tel: 028 9023 8645 www.nicem.org.uk	The Northern Ireland Pakistani Cultural Association, C/O 8 Braniel Park, Belfast, BT5 7JL Tel: 028 9083 6704	The Belfast Hebrew Congregation / Jewish Community, Katy Radford, C/O 9 Taunton Avenue, Belfast, BT15 4AD
The NI Hindu Cultural Centre and Temple, 86 Clifton Street, Belfast, BT13 1AB Tel: 028 9024 9746	Indian Community Centre, 86 Clifton St, Belfast, BT13 1AB, Tel 028 9024 9746	The Northern Ireland Filipino Association, C/O NICEM, 3rd Floor Ascot House, 24-31 Shaftesbury Square, Belfast, BT2 7DB Tel: 028 9023 8645
The Northern Ireland Sikh Cultural and Community Centre, 1 Simpson's Brae, Waterside, Londonderry, BT47 1DL Tel: 028 7134 3523		The Traveller Community, Belfast Travellers Educational and Development group, Site 12 – 2 Blackstaff Complex, 77 Springfield Road, Belfast BT12 7AE Tel: 028 9020 3337

RACE HATE ON RISE IN NI

With a racist attack in Northern Ireland almost every day, it has been dubbed the race-hate capital of Europe in some quarters. Some claim racism is replacing sectarianism in the province's post-Troubles society.

Ethnic minority groups have borne the brunt of attacks

Police statistics show 226 reported incidents of racism in the province in the 12 months up to March 2003. These include graffiti, verbal abuse and attacks. Police patrols have been stepped up in south Belfast where Chinese and Pakistani families, including pregnant women, have borne the brunt of recent attacks. Filipino nurses have also been targeted in Belfast and County Antrim and Muslim families have fled after attacks in County Armagh, where plans for the province's first mosque have been put on hold.

Three years ago, one of the most comprehensive studies into racial prejudice in the province indicated racism was twice as common as sectarianism. The University of Ulster interviewed 1,250 people and found "significant levels" of racism and anti-traveller prejudice. Two-thirds said they would not work with members of the travelling community, more than half would not accept travellers as neighbours and more than a third said they would not like to work with Asian, Afro-Caribbean or Chinese people.

A BBC investigation last October found that ethnic minorities in Northern Ireland were more than twice as likely to face a racist incident, than those in England or Wales.

"Those who carry out these appalling acts believe they act with sound reason",

Dr Gordon Gray, Presbyterian Church

Patrick Yu of the Northern Ireland Council for Ethnic Minorities said the recent spate of attacks could be the tip of the iceberg. "A lot of cases are not reported to the police for one reason or another, in particular they are more vulnerable to reprisal if they report them to the police," he said. "We need to educate people about the multi-culturalism now in Northern Ireland. We have more than two communities."

However, contrary to what the statistics would suggest, attitudes towards ethnic communities are not all negative. Perhaps this is typified by a newspaper in Dungannon which has begun a regular column in Portuguese and English to help the 1,500 Portuguese people who live and work in the area. Ian Greer, editor of the Tyrone Courier, said he wanted to help the migrant community feel involved in the life of the town: "The Portuguese are now a sizeable group that has come along in the past four to five years and is an important part of life in Dungannon."

'Race hate on rise in NI', BBC News, 13 January 2004, www.bbc.co.uk, accessed 2 April 2009

FOR YOUR FOLDER

1. What is the difference between prejudice and discrimination?

2. List the groups of people that face racist attacks in Northern Ireland.

3. Describe some of the ways they are attacked.

4. Describe the work of one organisation that opposes prejudice and discrimination.

WHAT THE BIBLE SAYS ABOUT RACISM

The Bible teaches that Christians should think carefully about how they treat others:

> *"Do for others what you want them to do for you"*
>
> Matthew 7:12

When Jesus met a Cannanite woman (ie, not a Jew), he put prejudice aside and healed her daughter:

> *"You are a woman of great faith! What you want will be done for you."*
>
> Matthew 15:21–28

Jesus based his teachings about other people on love:

> *"Love your neighbour as you love yourself."*
>
> Matthew 22:39

The Parable of the Good Samaritan is also concerned with racial injustice. Jesus told the parable when a man asked him: *"Who is my neighbour?"* At the time of Jesus, Jews and Samaritans hated each other. The story describes how a Jewish man was attacked and robbed on his way to Jericho. A priest and a Levite, both Jews, ignored the injured man and went on their way. When a Samaritan saw the injured man he put aside racial differences and took care of him:

> *"'In your opinion, which one of these three acted like a neighbor toward the man attacked by the robbers?' The teacher of the Law answered, 'The one who was kind to him.' Jesus replied, 'You go, then, and do the same.'"*
>
> Luke 10:36–37

The Story of Peter and Cornelius (Acts 10:1–48) is concerned with racial injustice. In its beginnings the early church was made up only of Jews, who still kept Jewish laws and traditions. When Gentiles (non-Jews) became Christians these Jews expected them to be faithful to the Jewish faith as well. Jews would not eat with Gentiles because they did not keep the Jewish food laws. This is an example of injustice.

Peter, a Jewish Christian and one of the original disciples, was challenged about holding such attitudes. Peter had a vision of a sheet that was full of all kinds of animals. Some of the animals were those that Jews were forbidden by the law to eat. However, God told Peter *"Do not call anything impure that God has made clean."* Peter realised that this was also to apply to people. Differences between Jews and Gentiles were not important to God because the gospel message was meant for everyone, without exception.

Paul's letters are clear on the equality of all people:

> *"So there is no difference between Jews and Gentiles, between slaves and free people, between men and women; you are all one in union with Christ Jesus."*
>
> Galatians 3:28

> *"there is no longer any distinction between Gentiles and Jews, circumcised and uncircumcised, barbarians, savages, slaves, and free, but Christ is all, Christ is in all."*
>
> Colossians 3:11

FOR YOUR FOLDER

Explain what the Parable of the Good Samaritan teaches Christians about their attitude towards people of a different race.

WHAT THE CHURCHES SAY ABOUT RACISM

The Roman Catholic Church strongly condemns racism:

> "The Church reproves, as foreign to the mind of Christ, any discrimination against people or any harassment of them on the basis of their race, colour, condition in life or religion."

Declaration on the Relation of the Church to non-Church religions (*Nostra Aetate*) Second Vatican Council, 1965

The Church of Ireland:

> "If we do not challenge the racism and discrimination that I fear could quickly gather pace in Ireland under the present political and economic circumstances, then how can we convince others that we believe in Christ and the Kingdom he proclaimed?"

Canon Patrick Comerford, Director of Spiritual Formation at the Church of Ireland Theological, Institute, 2008

Dr Ken Newell, former Moderator of **The Presbyterian Church** in Ireland on the subject of racism:

> "Become more socially inclusive. If you rarely have people from a different ethnic, religious or cultural backgrounds to your home for a meal, why not adopt a different approach? Open your heart and your home…There is nothing more powerful than your neighbours seeing you enjoy the friendship of people from different ethnic and racial backgrounds."

The Methodist Church:

> "We urge all Methodist people to be open to the diversity and enrichment that can come from people of different cultures, including those who have come to this island as refugees and asylum seekers. We deplore all forms of racism and seek to promote understanding and inclusion within church life and society in general. We encourage governments to show humanity, understanding, generosity and openness in their dealings with asylum seekers and refugees. We encourage local communities to welcome strangers to share in the life of this island."

Methodist Church in Ireland, Council on Social Responsibility

PRACTICAL WAYS THAT CHRISTIANS TRY TO COMBAT RACISM

hairy mary

In January 2008, at a Church of Ireland conference on immigration and integration Gerry Kelly, the Junior Minister in the Office of the First and Deputy First Minister for Northern Ireland, said that the Church had a key role in being able to deliver in areas where Government may not be able to.

> "The differences in our society must cease to be barriers. Difference must be recognised, appreciated and celebrated. It is important that we all act to make sure that intolerance, sectarianism, racism and violence have no place in our modern society. Every one of us has a responsibility and a role to play in creating a society that is at ease with the diversity of individuals and whole communities."

'Building a Welcoming Community', Newsletter Number 11, Spring 2008

All the churches in Ireland believe that it is important to build a welcoming community for newcomers and have responded in different ways. For example, in the Catholic Church each diocese in Ireland has a person in charge of the pastoral care of immigrants. And both the Presbyterian Church and the Methodist Church in Ireland have adopted a Policy on Asylum Seekers and Refugees which explores issues of immigration, racism and welcome. Other denominations have responded positively as well.

Churches can issue statements against racism but what can the ordinary Christian do to help? Some ideas include:

At Sunday worship services:

- The minister or priest can help the rest of the congregation to adjust to change by making them more aware of the cultures that newcomers belong to and persuading them of the importance of reaching out.

- Make sure the church building is welcoming from the outside, with clear welcoming signs.

- Have people responsible for welcoming at services and involve the whole congregation in learning about the importance of welcome. For example, it is helpful if people can be greeted with a phrase or two in their own language.

- Encourage newcomers to participate, for example, in reading a lesson or taking up the collection. These are small, visible signs of acceptance.

- Include some aspect of the worship tradition from the country of origin, such as a song or a prayer. Have songs of worship in a foreign language as well as in English.

- Hold special services, for example, in Refugee Week, Anti-Racism Sunday, or Holocaust Memorial Day, and invite members of minority groups to speak or attend.

Church premises during the week:

- Have drop-in centres or coffee mornings to give people the chance to mix.

- Hold mother and toddler groups for refugees or the families of migrant workers.

- Provide the chance for after-school clubs to help incoming children to adjust to the differences in the educational system.

- Help people with the learning of English.

- Use the churches recreational facilities, such as a sport's hall, to help people to make friends.

Day-to-day life

Christians are not just called to be welcoming within their congregations but also within their private lives and in their homes:

- Invite people from different ethnic, religious or cultural backgrounds to your home for a meal.

- Hold celebration meals, for example, at Christmas where you might invite people from a minority ethnic group to share their cooking traditions with you.

- Celebrate festivals such as Chinese New Year.

- Visit cultural centres in Northern Ireland together, for example, the Giant's Causeway, the Irish Linen Centre or the Ulster Folk and Transport Museum.

Giant's Causeway

Irish Linen Centre, Lisburn

Belfast Islamic Centre

- Visit the cultural centres of religious or ethnic communities – such as the Belfast Islamic Centre or the Indian Community Centre in Belfast, to learn, and affirm their presence as part of a shared society.

- Be careful about the words you use. Find out what people want to be called. For example, at one time 'coloured' was acceptable for African or Caribbean people. Now, in almost all cases, it is not.

- Be willing to study the languages, cultures and religions of people from minority ethnic populations.

Some of these suggestions were made by Rt Rev Dr Ken Newell, former Moderator of the Presbyterian Church in Ireland on the subject of racism [Lion&Lamb:racism and religious liberty, 'Live a Life of Love' Autumn 2004]

EMBRACE NI

Embrace NI is an inter-church organisation made up of a group of Christians in Northern Ireland who work together to promote a positive response to:

- people seeking asylum
- refugees
- migrant workers
- minority ethnic people

Its main role is to encourage church communities to make Northern Ireland a more welcoming place for all people from minority ethnic backgrounds. The official launch of EMBRACE took place in 2003 in Belfast. The Rev Arlington Trotman, Secretary of the Churches Together in Britain and Ireland Commission for Racial Justice, spoke at the launch, welcoming this initiative.
Find out more about EMBRACE
Web: www.embraceni.org

Information taken from EMBRACE NI, www.embraceni.org, accessed 12 November 2008

FURTHER THINKING

Find out about the work of the following groups:

- **Evangelical Alliance:** www.eauk.org/northern-ireland
- **Centre for Contemporary Christianity in Ireland (CCCI) (formerly ECONI)** www.contemporarychristianity.org
- **The Corrymeela Community** www.corrymeela.org
- **Churches Together in Britain and Ireland (CTBI)** www.ctbi.org.uk
- **The Churches' Commission for Racial Justice (CCRJ)** www.ctbi.org.uk/ccrj

FOR YOUR FOLDER

1. How might the Bible influence a Christian's attitude towards racism?

2. Make a list of the practical things a church can do to help a person from an ethnic minority feel welcome?

3. Do you think the Church does enough to help people facing racist attacks?

4. "In Northern Ireland Christians should concentrate on healing the divide between Catholics and Protestants. Racism is not really a big problem." How would you respond to this statement?

CHRISTIAN ATTITUDES TOWARDS OTHER RELIGIONS

Christian attitudes towards other religions are often referred to as working for 'inter-faith understanding'. The term 'inter-faith' sometimes refers to inter-denominational relationships within Christianity but it can also be applied to the relationship between Christians and members of other world faiths. Christians vary in their attitudes towards other religions, depending on their own beliefs. Some feel that there are many ways to God and accept that other religions are just as important as their own. Others believe that non-Christian religions may hold some truths but that Christianity is the only true religion. These different attitudes are reflected in the extent to which Christians are prepared to come together with those of other faiths.

For some Christians, diversity is a cause for celebration and they are keen to learn about different faiths and cultures. For others there is suspicion and a feeling that the churches should be mindful of what is unique to Christianity. In extreme cases the existence of different faiths in Northern Ireland causes unease, friction and conflict.

Why is it important for Christians to have a positive attitude to other world religions?

1. The world is becoming increasingly secular, with many people opting to have no religious faith at all. Some Christians feel that a lack of faith in the world has led to a decrease in moral values. It is argued that this is a good reason for people of all faiths to come together. They feel there should be more opportunities to meet with those of other faiths to present a common approach to moral and social issues such as poverty, oppression and violence. Francis Campbell, Ambassador to the Vatican comments:

   > "The separation in the world is increasingly not between faiths and subdivisions of faith but between faith and the lack of it. How to respond to rapid social change while staying faithful to tradition is a challenge for all faiths."

2. In recent years more and more people who live in Northern Ireland are from different cultural and religious backgrounds. It is important to get on with your neighbour. Christians believe it is useful to learn more about each other in order to promote a more harmonious society.

INTERFAITH DIALOGUE AND THE CHURCHES

Over the past 25 years or so, all the main churches have been involved in a range of inter-faith activity. This has included showing hospitality to minority communities, being there for other faiths in times of crisis, and developing dialogue with one or more religions. The emphasis has focused on Christians being involved with people of other faiths without trying to convert them. Some of the main Christian denominations have produced guidelines for inter-faith dialogue, such as the Church of Ireland (written by Canon Patrick Comerford).

IN A GROUP

Discuss why some Christians may be reluctant to take part in dialogue with people from other world faiths.

NORTHERN IRELAND INTER-FAITH FORUM

The Northern Ireland Inter-Faith Forum (NIIFF) was formed in May 1993, following discussion with members of the ethnic and religious communities in Northern Ireland. The Forum provides a safe place for members of different faiths to meet.

The main aims of the Forum:

- To promote mutual understanding between different faith traditions.

- To educate people that Northern Ireland is not a country of two traditions only, but a vibrant community of many faiths, whose people come from varied religious and ethnic backgrounds.

The Forum meets four times a year. Some of the activities carried out include talks and discussion;

special presentations; visits to community centres and places of worship; and meeting socially. The work of the Inter-Faith Forum has been successful in terms of creating new friendships and the recognition of the rich diversity of community and cultural life in Northern Ireland.

You may already be familiar with some of the work carried out by the Inter-Faith Forum; for example:

- A major exhibition, 'In Good Faith', which travelled around Northern Ireland, to demonstrate its rich variety of religious life.

- A series of annual multi-faith calendars distributed to schools. There may be one displayed in your classroom.

- Visits to schools, colleges and faith communities to talk about various faith traditions.

- The establishment and maintenance of The Quiet Room at Belfast International Airport, which provides a space for reflection and prayer for all.

FOR YOUR FOLDER

1. Name some world faiths other than Christianity.

2. What is meant by "inter-faith understanding"?

3. Describe the work of the Inter-Faith Forum.

4. Do you think it important for Christians to have a positive attitude to other world religions?

● RELIGIOUS DIVERSITY IN SCHOOLS

Northern Ireland, along with the rest of the UK and Ireland, includes Religious Studies (RS) in its curriculum. In 1993 the Core Syllabus for Religious Studies was agreed by representatives of the main Christian denominations. It was decided that the syllabus would be a 'Christian' syllabus. Some people were very unhappy that the existence of

other religions in Northern Ireland seemed to have been ignored. They argued that there was a need for inclusion, respect, and fairness to all religions and to those people who have no faith at all. Others feared that a study of world religions would confuse children about their own faith. Ten years later the Core Syllabus for Religious Studies was revised. The study of world religions is now studied at Key Stage 3. Most of you will have studied at least one world religion at school already.

Read the following comments by teenagers about the place of world religions in Religious Studies:

"If we study other religions, people can find out if what they're saying is going to offend someone."

"It helps you to learn how to interact with different faiths within our society."

"I think we shouldn't have to because if we don't believe in these faiths why do we need to learn about them. It would be confusing and what if someone decided they wanted to change religion. Wouldn't the school be in trouble?"

"Learning about them might stop some racism as people will start to respect the religions."

"Yes I think you should because my friend is a Muslim and he always left the classroom when we had RS. We never learned anything about his religion and I would have liked to know about it."

"It stops people thinking that their religion is the only way to get to God."

IN A GROUP

Do you think schools should teach about religions other than Christianity?

Draw a table and list 'arguments for' in one column and 'arguments against' in another.

THE PLACE OF THE CHRISTIAN ACT OF WORSHIP IN SCHOOL ASSEMBLY

In 1944 it was made law for children to pray at school everyday. Schools in Northern Ireland hold an act of Christian worship, like assembly or prayers, every day. Many of you will have been to Assembly this morning. There may have been a Bible reading or a hymn. Perhaps you all said the Lord's Prayer. You may not think very much about this because you are used to it and it is part of your daily routine in school.

Schools in the UK, especially in England, have changed a lot since 1944 and now have children from lots of different religions. Some people argue that it is not right for schools to have this daily act of Christian worship. They say that it makes pupils from other religions feel excluded and makes them stand out as being different. How do you think a Muslim pupil feels standing in a hall where everyone around them is saying a Christian prayer?

Some think that the rule is outdated and that it should be up to schools to decide how and when they pray. Others argue that other religions should be represented at school assemblies. It is not as big an issue in Northern Ireland as it is in England as the majority of pupils in schools here are associated with the Christian religion. However, it may become more of an issue in the future as more people from other religions move to Northern Ireland.

FOR YOUR FOLDER

Describe what happened in your school assembly this morning.

Do you think that school assembly should be made more welcoming for pupils of other religions? If so, how might this be achieved?

THE ISSUE OF RELIGIOUS DRESS AND SCHOOL UNIFORM

Read the following real life stories:

1. Shabina Begumi, 15, attended a school in England where more than 75% of the pupils

were Muslims. Her school banned her from wearing traditional Muslim clothes, the head-to-toe dress, called a jilbab, to lessons. The school was willing for Shabina to wear other traditional Muslim clothing – trousers and tunic, called a shalwar kameez but they regarded the jilbab as a safety risk. Shabina's lawyer explained that the jilbab was recognised by many Muslims as a requirement for their religion. Shabina argued that she was being stopped from practising her religious beliefs and getting an education.

The case went to court three times, but the House of Lords backed the school's right to bring in the ban. They said the school had gone to great lengths to come up with a uniform policy which respected Muslim beliefs.

Shabina said she was disappointed, but said she was glad it was all over and that she could now move on: "I'm just a teenager – not many teenagers go out there and challenge the system."

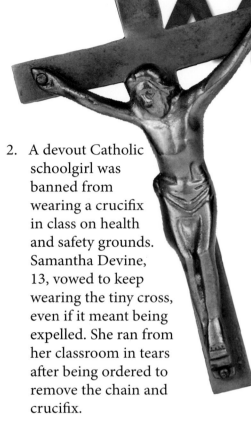

2. A devout Catholic schoolgirl was banned from wearing a crucifix in class on health and safety grounds. Samantha Devine, 13, vowed to keep wearing the tiny cross, even if it meant being expelled. She ran from her classroom in tears after being ordered to remove the chain and crucifix.

"I am proud of my religion and it is my right to wear a cross around my neck," she said yesterday. "I can't understand why the school thinks a tiny crucifix on a thin silver necklace is a health and safety hazard." Her mother also commented:
"I was brought up to be proud of my religion and we believe it is our daughter's right to be proud of what she believes in and wear a symbol of her faith."

Some people argue that the wearing of religious dress or symbols in schools is divisive and draws attention to our differences. In France, all religious symbols are banned in schools. Do you think people should be allowed to wear what they want in schools? Or do you think everyone should be dressed the same, no matter what their religion?

THE CONTRIBUTION OF RELIGION TO COMMUNITY COHESION

Throughout this chapter you have seen how religion can contribute to problems in our community. However, religion also has a positive role to play in bringing the community together and contributing to community cohesion. The word 'cohesion' means 'pulling together'. So putting religious differences aside, there are many people in society who want to work together for a better future.

'Reconciliation' is a key word for community cohesion. It is a process through which people can try to work through their negative attitudes towards others. For example, with the issue of racism, some people, such as members of EMBRACE NI have devoted their lives to making a difference. Other ways that Christians can contribute to community cohesion is by being involved in charity work. One example is seen in the work of Catholic charity The Society of St Vincent de Paul.

The Society of St Vincent de Paul has been helping to alleviate poverty and working for social justice in Northern Ireland since 1848. The aim of the Society is:

> "to enhance the quality of life for those in need, regardless of creed, colour or caste."

The society is also concerned with giving practical support to those experiencing social exclusion, by providing a wide range of services to people in need. Members believe that people do not just need financial help and so visiting the sick, the lonely and the imprisoned forms a large proportion of the society's work.

Members work on a voluntary basis through 179 branches spread throughout Northern Ireland. Volunteers offer friendship, support, advice and practical help to families, pensioners and individuals each week. Some examples of the services offered by St Vincent de Paul include:

- Cash assistance
- Food and clothing
- Shops and internet cafes
- Furniture stores
- Breakfast and afterschool clubs
- Creches
- Playgroups
- Mother and toddler group
- Centre for the Deaf (Belfast)
- Drop-in-centres
- Resource centres
- Providing accommodation to vulnerable people
- Holiday schemes and Holiday Home (Newcastle)

FOR YOUR FOLDER

1. Why might some Christians disagree with the teaching of world religions in schools?

2. Explain why schools in the UK have a Christian Act of Worship in Assembly?

3. Do you think that pupils in schools should be allowed to wear religious symbols, even if they are a health and safety hazard?

4. Describe some of the ways that Christians contribute to community cohesion.

FURTHER THINKING

Find out about some of the other communities that have been formed in Northern Ireland and which contribute to community cohesion.

- **The Corrymeela Community** www.corrymeela.org
- **The Clonard/Fitzroy Fellowship** www.fitzroy.org.uk/articles
- **The Curragh Community** www.ccommunity.fsnet.co.uk
- **The Cornerstone Community** www.cornerstonecom.fsnet.co.uk

Chapter 5

WAR AND PEACE

● PACIFISM

Pacifism is the belief that war and violence are wrong and cannot be justified. Pacifists believe that conflicts should be settled by peaceful means. This may also involve positive action to promote justice and human rights.

There are different levels of pacifism depending on how strongly a person feels about war.

LEVELS OF PACIFISM	
Absolute pacifism	An absolute pacifist believes that it is never right to take part in war, even in self-defence. Human life is so precious that nothing can justify deliberately killing a person.
Conditional pacifism	A conditional pacifist is against the idea of war in general, but accepts that sometimes there may be extreme circumstances when war is better than the alternative.
Selective pacifism	A selective pacifist opposes only a certain type of war, such as one that involves weapons of mass destruction, for example, nuclear weapons.

Some pacifists take the line that doing nothing is the best course of action. Others believe that they can take action to bring about change or to resist oppression by non-violent means. They are closely involved in political activity to promote peace. They argue that there are non-violent methods they can use to convince the enemy that their point of view is right. Some of these methods include:

- Peaceful demonstrations
- Strikes in places of work
- Road blocks
- Picketing
- Hunger strikes

There are also laws that allow people to refuse to fight if they believe that it is the wrong thing to do. Such people are called 'conscientious objectors'.

FURTHER THINKING

Statue of Mahatma Gandhi in Union Square NYC

One of the most famous leaders of a non-violent movement was Gandhi (1869–1948). He opposed British rule in India during the twentieth century. Gandhi took the religious principle of doing no harm (common to Buddhism and Hinduism) and turned it into a non-violent tool for action. His view on conflict is summed up in his famous statement: "An eye for an eye and the world will all soon be blind." Find out how Gandhi used the method of non-violence.

WHAT THE BIBLE SAYS ABOUT PACIFISM

The Bible tends to teach that war and violence are wrong and to be avoided. In the Old Testament the Psalmist expressed the need for peace:

> "Turn away from evil and do good; strive for peace with all your heart."
>
> Psalm 34:14

This teaching is further emphasised in the New Testament:

> "You have heard that it was said, 'An eye for an eye, and a tooth for a tooth.' But now I tell you: do not take revenge on someone who wrongs you. If anyone slaps you on the right cheek, let him slap your left cheek too."
>
> Matthew 5:38–39

Christians generally agree that it is wrong to be involved in war and they look to the life of Jesus for an example of how to act. Jesus adopted a middle ground. On the one hand, his words promote peace:

> "Happy are those who work for peace; God will call them his children!"
>
> Matthew 5:9

> "Love your enemies and pray for those who persecute you."
>
> Matthew 5:44

> "…live in peace with one another."
>
> Mark 9:50

In the last week of his life when the soldiers came to arrest Jesus one of disciples drew a sword and Jesus told him to put it away. He healed the man and made it clear that violence was not the way forward:

> "All who take the sword will die by the sword."
>
> Matthew 26:51–55

Similarly in his letters, Paul agrees with the teaching of Jesus:

> "If someone has done you wrong, do not repay him with a wrong…Do not let evil defeat you; instead, conquer evil with good."
>
> Romans 12:17–21

WHAT THE CHURCHES SAY ABOUT PACIFISM

All Christians want peace and many Christians are pacifists, but some accept that war is inevitable. You may find it surprising that none of the major Christian churches adopts a total pacifist approach.

However, one group of Christians, the Quakers (Religious Society of Friends), is well known for their views in support of pacifism:

> "We utterly deny all outward wars and strife, and fightings with outward weapons, for any end, or under any pretence whatever; this is our testimony to the whole world."
>
> A Declaration given to King Charles II, 1660

Quakers refuse to join the army but they do help out in times of war by acting as medics, driving ambulances or taking part in relief work.

Other Christian denominations are more open to the inevitability of war:

> "The Christian pacifist does not necessarily condemn the use of every kind of force, but refuses to employ force unnecessarily or to destroy others, for example either in personal or state violence."

The Methodist Church

In history Christians have been known to fight for God. For example, in the Crusades Christians fought against the Muslims. Many Christians also accept the concept of a Just War. The criteria for a Just War were actually devised by Christians. However, most Christians still regard war as a last resort.

The Catholic Church gives more practical advice about how to avoid wars. For example, it argues that "nuclear weapons should be banned."

WHAT OTHER WORLD FAITHS SAY ABOUT PACIFISM

Among other world faiths there are similar views about war and pacifism. In general Judaism is strongly opposed to violence. If it is needed then only the minimum amount of force should be used. Jewish law does accept that sometimes violence may be the only solution. Jews have a moral obligation to save the life of a person who is under attack, even if the solution is to kill the attacker. Jewish law also allows Jews to use violence on the Sabbath in response to an invasion.

Most Buddhists are pacifists. At the heart of Buddhism is the principle of non-harming, *ahimsa*. The first of the five moral precepts, which Buddhists keep, is to abstain from taking life.

> "Hence Buddhism is a religion of love, understanding and compassion, and committed towards the ideal of non-violence."

The Buddhist Declaration on Nature

THE DEBATE ABOUT PACIFISM	
Some arguments for pacifism	Some arguments against pacifism
• Belief in the sanctity of life. • Religious faith. • Belief that war is wasteful.	• A state has a duty to protect its citizens, and its citizens have a moral duty to carry out certain tasks in war. • The Bible allows war.

'Non-Violence', known as 'The Knotted Gun', a sculpture by Cark Fredrik Reutersward, a gift from the government of Luxembourg to the United Nations.

FOR YOUR FOLDER

1. What is a pacifist?

2. Describe some of the positive things a pacifist can do during war time without taking part in fighting.

3. Explain why some Christians might refuse to fight in a war.

4. Do you think that the best way for a Christian to work for peace is to be a pacifist?

● WAR

A war is an attempt by one state to either:

- defend itself against another state

  or

- to try to take something, such as land, resources or freedom, from another power.

WHAT THE BIBLE SAYS ABOUT WAR

The Bible speaks of how **war is inevitable**:

"Everything that happens in this world happens at the time God chooses…the time for killing and the time for healing, the time for tearing down and the time for building…the time for love and the time for hate, the time for war and the time for peace."

Ecclesiastes 3:1, 3 & 8

"The end will come like a flood, bringing the war and destruction which God has prepared."

Daniel 9:26

Jesus himself said:

"You are going to hear the noise of battles close by and the news of battles far away; but do not be troubled. Such things must happen, but they do not mean that the end has come. Countries will fight each other; kingdoms will attack one another. There will be famines and earthquakes everywhere. All these things are like the first pains of childbirth."

Matthew 24:6–8

"Do not think that I have come to bring peace to the world. No, I did not come to bring peace, but a sword. I came to set sons against their fathers, daughters against their mothers, daughters-in-law against their mothers-in-law; your worst enemies will be the members of your own family."

Matthew 10:34–36

Christians believe it is always with justice that God judges and makes war:

"it is with justice that he judges and fights his battles."

Revelation 19:11

However, it is only right to go to war when it is **the will of God**:

But Moses said, "Why are you disobeying the Lord's command? This will not succeed! Do not go up, because the Lord is not with you. You will be defeated by your enemies, for the Amalekites and Canaanites will face you there. Because you have turned away from the Lord, he will not be with you and you will fall by the sword."

Numbers 14:41–43

FOR YOUR FOLDER

1. The Old Testament is full of examples of how God used his people in war to bring judgment on nations who had sinned against him. Look up the following references and list the examples:

- **Genesis 15:16**
- **Numbers 21:3**
- **Numbers 31:1–7**
- **Numbers 32:20-21**
- **Deuteronomy 7:1–2**
- **Joshua 6:20–21**
- **Joshua 8:1–8**
- **Joshua 10:29–32**
- **Joshua 11:7–20**

2. How do you think the Old Testament and the New Testament differ in their attitudes to violence and war?

HOLY WARS

Christians often view the idea of a Holy War as a contradiction in terms. How can a war be called 'holy'? Killing people and causing destruction seems to have nothing to do with holiness. However, religion and war are often linked. Many soldiers go to war believing that God is with them and is on their side.

Holy wars are usually:

- called for by a religious leader or authority, such as the Church. In the Old Testament there are several occasions where God directed his people to wage war.
- fought to achieve a religious goal, such as to spread the faith or to rescue believers.
- expected to give a spiritual reward for those who take part.

The Crusades

From AD1095 until AD1291 there was a series of Christian holy wars called the Crusades. The aim of these wars was to capture the Christian sacred places in the Holy Land from the Muslims who lived there.

The first Crusade was started by Pope Urban II in 1095. Furious at the capture of the holy places, he ordered a war to restore Christianity. He believed the war would have the support of God. They captured Jerusalem and the people of the city were slaughtered by the Christian invaders.

RICHARD CŒUR DE LION AND SALADIN.

WHAT IS THE DIFFERENCE BETWEEN A HOLY WAR AND A JUST WAR?

A Holy War is fought to protect the religion of the people concerned. A 'Just War' is fought for any reason that is justified. The country that wants to go to war must demonstrate that there is a 'just' cause to do so.

Just War is a mainly Christian theory* which begins with the belief that taking human life is wrong. However, it holds that countries do have a duty to protect and defend their citizens. In some extreme cases this means being willing to use force.

*Although it is used by people of every faith or none.

Which of these statements do you agree with?

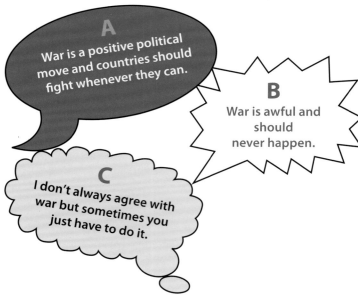

A
War is a positive political move and countries should fight whenever they can.

B
War is awful and should never happen.

C
I don't always agree with war but sometimes you just have to do it.

A **supports war** and is probably not held by many people.

B is an example of **Pacifism**

C is the basis of the **Just War tradition.**

THE JUST WAR TRADITION

There are two questions a country may need to ask if it is under threat of attack:

1. Is it just to go to war?
2. How should such a war be fought?

The purpose of the Just War theory is to guide a state when faced with potential threat and conflict situations. It is to help it to decide if it should go to war. The theory shows that war is wrong, except in exceptional circumstances and that a just cause must be evident.

JUST CAUSE

A war should be fought only for a cause that is **morally justified**. Before going to war a state must prove that there is a 'just cause' to do so. A just cause may be:

- in self-defence against an enemy's attack
- to defend the innocent
- to prevent an anticipated attack by a potential enemy
- to help a neighbour state that has been attacked

Can you think of any other reasons?

CRITERIA FOR A JUST WAR

St Thomas Aquinas suggested that there were conditions or criteria that had to be met before a war could be declared 'just' and it was fine to fight in such a war. Many people believe that it is right to go to war if it is just.

1. War must be the last resort. All other possibilities of settling the problem should be tried, for example, negotiation, or withdrawal of financial aid. The Charter of the United Nations states that short of actual attack, "all Members shall settle their international disputes by peaceful means" (Article 2:3).

2. War must be lawfully declared by a government with the authority to declare war. 'Ordinary' people or even terrorists like Osama Bin Laden could not declare a Just War.

3. There must be a just cause and proper intention for the war, such as keeping peace or defending the innocent.

4. There must be a reasonable chance of success.

5. The good gained by winning the war must be greater than the evil caused by fighting it.

6. There must be proportionality. Only 'appropriate' force should be used. If someone throws a stone at you, killing their whole family is not just. The same principle applies here.

7. Innocent civilians should not be killed.

8. Peace must be restored at the end.

WHAT THE CHURCHES SAY ABOUT JUST WAR

The Roman Catholic Church supports a Just War:

> "While the danger of war remains… Governments cannot be denied the right to defence if they have exhausted every peaceful means of settlement."
>
> *Gaudum et Spes*

They define a just cause:

> "Force may be used only to correct a grave, public evil, ie, aggression or massive violation of the basic rights of whole populations."
>
> US Catholic Conference 1993

Some Christians are totally opposed to the idea of a Just War. They believe that all war is unjust. They argue that accepting the Just War theory is saying that violence is acceptable.

IN A GROUP

1. Give two conditions or criteria for a Just War.
2. How do Christian denominations differ when it comes to Just War?
3. How is a Just War different from a Holy War?
4. Explain why some Christians might decide to fight in a war.

The war in Iraq: joint statement by religious leaders

"We have gathered against the backdrop of military action in Iraq involving British forces. They, their families and everyone caught up in this conflict are in our thoughts and prayers – especially those whose lives or loved ones have been lost.

As religious leaders from several faiths, we are here to signal the common ground on which we stand and to reaffirm the values we share at this time of tension, conflict and discord.

We pray that almighty God will grant wisdom, judgment and compassion to the political and military leaders who carry the immense burden of responsibility for the way this war is prosecuted.

Respect for every human being in times of armed conflict, as set out in the Geneva conventions and protocols, must be guaranteed on all sides. The rights and needs of civilians innocently affected by the conflict must be fully protected.

This is a conflict neither about religion nor between religions. We completely reject any attempt to misrepresent it in this way. As Christian, Jewish and Muslim religious leaders in this country, we believe that it is vital, amid so much uncertainty and turmoil, to resist any attempt to drive our communities apart.

We commend the continuing efforts being made in Britain to build a society in which different faith communities can flourish side-by-side in mutual respect and harmony.

We urge all communities to maintain their commitment to this goal, at a time when it may come under strain. We commit ourselves fully to strive to that end, for the sake of our shared well-being and as a mark of our commitment to a more harmonious, less conflict-ridden world.

Although, sadly, the diplomatic road is currently blocked, military action can only be a limited means to an end. We pray that early efforts to achieve a just, lasting and secure peace both in Iraq and throughout the Middle East may follow swiftly in the footsteps of war. We urge those with the power to help make real this vision, to remain true, amid the clamour of conflict, to that noble and vital purpose.

It is a vision which we commend in the confident belief that by so doing we are acting in the true interests of our God given humanity."

This joint statement was been issued by: Dr Rowan Williams, The Archbishop of Canterbury; Cardinal Cormac Murphy-O'Connor, Archbishop of Westminster; Revd David Coffey, The Free Churches Moderator; Dr Jonathan Sacks, The Chief Rabbi; Shaikh Dr Zaki Badawi, Chairman of the Council of Mosques and Imams UK; Reverend Esme Beswick, Co-President of Churches Together in England.

IN A GROUP

THE WAR IN IRAQ – A JUST WAR?
Look at the statement made by religious leaders on the war in Iraq. Draw a two-column table. Research the war in Iraq. On the left side, write out the conditions for a Just War. On the right side, next to each condition, say whether you think that the war against Iraq fulfils these criteria. Give evidence for what you think.

Do you think there is a danger that the Just War theory can lead people to believe that war is acceptable?

Index